**From Field to Court, from Ring to Diamond—
Great Moments That Will Live Forever in Shame!**

Q: What did a Canadian soccer team get when it traded one of its players?

A: A soccer ball.

Q: Why was jockey Willie Shoemaker's Kentucky Derby celebration a colossal foul-up?

A: He hadn't crossed the finish linc.

Q: How did football wide receiver Rick Eber make great catches?

A: By taping tacks to his hands.

Q: How did Roberto De Vicenzo lose the 1968 Masters Golf Tournament?

A: He made a mistake on his scorecard.

Q: What two National Hockey League teams ran up a total of 406 penalty minutes in one game?

A: The Boston Bruins and the Minnesota Northstars.

Q: In 1978 a racing greyhound at Hollywood, Florida, finally caught the mechanical rabbit. How?

A: He reversed directions and ambushed the rabbit from the front.

Q: Why did Kia Sladeski have to give up her American Rodeo Association's Rookie Cowgirl of the Year award?

A: *She* was a *he*.

Q: Why was a 1928 goal scored in the English "Wall Game" so unusual?

A: It was the first goal scored in fifty years.

THE
SPORTS HALL
OF
SHAME™

By Bruce Nash and Allan Zullo
Bernie Ward, Curator

POCKET BOOKS

New York   London   Toronto   Sydney   Tokyo

This book is dedicated to two great sports, Sophie Nash and Kathy Zullo . . . and to anyone who has ever hooked a drive into the next fairway, tossed back-to-back 7-10 splits, lost a tennis match on a double fault, or committed an equally inglorious screw-up on the field of play.

An *Original* Publication of POCKET BOOKS

POCKET BOOKS, a division of Simon & Schuster Inc.
1230 Avenue of the Americas, New York, NY 10020

ISBN: 0-671-63387-2

First-Pocket Books trade paperback printing October 1987

10   9   8   7   6   5   4

THE SPORTS HALL OF SHAME is a registered trademark
of Nash and Zullo Productions, Inc.

POCKET and colophon are trademarks of
Simon & Schuster Inc.

Printed in the U.S.A.

CONTENTS

ACKNOWLEDGMENTS

We wish to thank all the fans, athletes, coaches, and sportswriters who contributed nominations.

We are especially grateful to those athletes, past and present, who shared a few laughs with us as they recounted the outrageous moments that earned them a place in The Sports Hall of SHAME.

This book couldn't have been completed without the outstanding research efforts of Al Kermisch. We also appreciate the special efforts of Dusty Brandel, American Auto Racing Writers and Broadcasters Association; Fritz Brennecke; Bob Cicero; Dick Cohen, Sports Bookshelf; Camil Derouches, Montreal Canadiens; Jim Dressel, editor, *Bowlers Journal;* Fred Duckett; F.P.E. Gardner, professor, Eton College, London; Nick Gates, sports editor, *Knoxville Journal;* Max Grizzard; Fred Grossman, editor, *Daily Racing Form;* John Halligan, New York Rangers; Randy Heath; Hiram Henriquez; Billy House; W. Lloyd Johnson, executive director, Society for American Baseball Research; Hank Kaplan, boxing historian; Bill Kiser, National Motorsports Press Association; Ladies Professional Bowling Tour; Dave Lancer, PGA Tour; Jeff Letoffski; Jerry Levine; Bernie Manhoff, National Veteran Boxers Association; Valarie McGonigle, Atlantic City Race Track; Dick Mittman, *Indianapolis News;* Don Naman, Alabama International Motor Speedway; Dave Phillips, major league umpire and director of officiating, Missouri Valley Conference; Bruce Pluckhahn, curator, National Bowling Hall of Fame and Museum; Pro Bowlers Association; Bob Robinson, *Portland Oregonian;* Carmen Salvino; Beth Shetzeley, U.S. Tennis Association; Luke Soler; Glen Stout, Boston Public Library; Jerry Tapp, associate editor, *Referee* magazine; Steve Waid, *Grand National Scene;* David Wallechinsky, author *The Complete Book of the Olympics;* Joe Whitlock, Motor Sports, Inc.; Tim Williams, NFL Alumni Association; and Howard Willman, *Track & Field News.*

Our lineup wouldn't be such a winner without our rookies, Robyn and Jennifer Nash and Allison and Sasha Zullo.

THE SHAME GAME

After paying a lighthearted tribute to the national pastime in three volumes of *The Baseball Hall of SHAME* and to America's favorite spectator sport in *The Football Hall of SHAME,* we knew we couldn't stop chronicling hilarious happenings and ignoble incidents. We had a duty—an obligation—to go beyond the diamond and gridiron to document other outrageous sports moments and preserve them in the ultimate shrine of shrines: The Sports Hall of SHAME.

Let's face it, baseball and football don't have an exclusive license to shame. We found plenty of bloopers, blunders, and buffoonery on the courts, on the ice and in the ring, on the fairways and straightaways, in alleys, on tracks, at high schools and the Olympics. But we haven't forgotten baseball and football in this book. Since these two sports continue to provide fans with wacky moments, we have included chapters detailing a new slate of players inducted into The Baseball and Football Halls of SHAME.

Some of The Sports Hall of SHAME inductees—and many of our readers—have asked us if we plan to erect our own Hall of SHAME building. We're trying to find an appropriate site for our shrine, a place that best reflects what we stand for. Among the suggestions we're considering are Embarrass, Minnesota, and Defeated, Tennessee. We're also looking into the possibility of buying a parcel of land to incorporate into a burg called Blooperstown.

We envision a tacky and garish shrine that would display some of the mementoes of incidents highlighted in *The Sports Hall of SHAME.* We could show off the thumbtacks that helped pro receiver Rick Eber catch passes; the basketball that the Sacramento Kings couldn't score a hoop with during an entire period; one of the octopuses thrown onto the ice in a bizarre ritual of Detroit Red Wing fans; the dress that tennis player Linda Siegel fell out of during her Wimbledon match; the boxing gloves worn by Joseph "Ace" Falu, whose entire ring career lasted fourteen seconds; one of the wheels that flew off racer David Pearson's car when he left the pit too soon; the ball that pro bowler Palmer Fallgren dented the ceiling with; the uniform worn by outfielder Mel Hall when it snagged on a wire fence and hung him up; and the skis that flew off the feet of jumper Chuck Ryan in midflight.

Meanwhile, we will continue to chronicle the rib-tickling, embarrassing moments in sports as they happen. We won't play favorites. We will continue to dishonor both the heroes and the zeroes. As our motto says, "Fame *and* shame are part of the game."

THE BASKETBALL
HALL OF SHAME

Derek Harper

Guard ■ Dallas Mavericks ■ May 6, 1984

Teams usually score a combined total of more than two hundred points in an NBA game. So what's the big deal if a player loses track of just one? Ask Derek Harper.

In a crucial 1984 play-off game against the Los Angeles Lakers, the Dallas Mavericks' rookie guard thought his team was ahead by a point. He dribbled the final six seconds off the clock and then began celebrating—until he was told to look at the scoreboard. The score was tied 108–108! His blunder sent the game into overtime, where the Lakers ripped the Mavericks 122–115. By taking an insurmountable three-games-to-one lead, L.A. went on to win the play-off series.

Playing at home against the favored Lakers, the Mavericks desperately needed a victory to even the play-off series at two wins apiece. In the nip-and-tuck battle, Dallas center Pat Cummings tied the score at 108 when he sank a left-handed hook shot with thirty-one seconds left and was fouled by Magic Johnson.

With no timeouts left for the Mavericks, Harper conferred with coach Dick Motta while Cummings shot the free throw that would have given Dallas the lead. Cummings missed, but unexplainably Harper assumed his teammate had made the foul shot to put the Mavericks ahead 109–108.

The Lakers rebounded the missed free throw and worked the ball in to Kareem Abdul-Jabbar, who missed a sky hook. Dallas grabbed the rebound with time to get off one shot or at least try to draw the foul. The Mavericks pushed the ball up the court and passed to Harper, who dribbled unhindered forty feet from the basket. At the buzzer he began celebrating what he thought was the team's biggest victory in its short four-year history. The unblinking eye of national television relayed Harper's horror when he realized he had screwed up royally. They needed a crane to pick up his jaw.

Motta, who tried everything to alert Harper, said afterward, "When I saw Derek backing up, it hit me that he didn't know the score or the time. I wanted to tackle him. Would they call a foul on a coach for tackling one of his players?"

Added Los Angeles coach Pat Riley, "I was as surprised as anybody when Harper didn't go in. Why, I was about to call a play for him myself."

When a mob of reporters rushed his locker after the game, Harper said, "I'll take the blame for the loss. It was a mistake. I thought we were ahead."

The way Harper works with numbers, it's a good bet he'd never land a job as an accountant.

Brian Williams

Guard ■ University of Cincinnati ■ January 19, 1977

It was bad enough for Brian Williams when he missed the entire basket on a slam dunk. Even worse, he missed the hoop *and* wound up hitting an official squarely on the head!

The 6-foot, 5-inch University of Cincinnati guard made the most deplorable dunk in college basketball history during a game against the University of Louisville.

"I've seen some missed dunks, but never one where a referee got conked," recalled Williams's coach, Gale Catlett. "Brian really nailed him. That official staggered all over the court for at least a couple of minutes."

The visiting Bearcats, then rated No. 2 in the nation, were trailing Louisville by six points with two minutes to go in the game when Williams soared down the lane and launched himself for what looked like a dramatic slam dunk. Meanwhile, referee Darwin Brown positioned himself under the basket.

Williams sailed high in the air, held the ball straight over his head and then slammed it down—only to miss both the rim and the backboard. In fact, he missed everything—except the referee. The ball smashed into Brown's head and ricocheted crazily into the seats.

"The crowd loved it, but I damn near got knocked out," Brown recalled. "I staggered around and had the same thought as everyone else—how could he miss the basket like that?"

Chuck Connors

Center ■ Boston Celtics ■ November 5, 1946

Chuck Connors made a smashing debut in front of bleachers full of Boston Celtics fans during the team's very first home game. He shattered the glass backboard.

Long before he achieved fame as the star of the TV series "The Rifleman," Connors was a pro basketball player who made Boston's roster as a center in 1946, the team's first season.

Connors rifling a pass after his smashing debut   Courtesy Chuck Connors

At the Celtics' home opener, more than 4,000 fans crowded into the Boston Arena to see the league's newest team take on the Chicago Stags. The spectators didn't know all the Celtics; however, they soon took special note of the squad's 6-foot, 5-inch center.

During pregame warmups, just five minutes before the tip-off, Connors tossed up a shot that hit the rim of the basket. The backboard leaned forward and then spider-webbed into a million pieces.

Arena officials had to race over to the Boston Garden and borrow one of its backboards. By the time the replacement was set up at the Arena, the game had been delayed for more than an hour.

"The crowd got pretty fidgety after a while and [Celtics coach] Honey Russell was incensed," recalled Connors. "Boy, did he let me have it. He shouted, 'Damn it, Connors, every time you're around me, something bad happens!' I told him, 'It was just a set shot and it's not really my fault.' And he replied, 'You threw it up there, didn't you?' He just jumped all over me and the longer it took to get a new backboard, the madder he got.

"Of all the times for it to happen, it had to be at the very first Celtics game. They had been ballyhooing the new team and the game, and of course the fans were all excited. Then I had to break the backboard. There I was standing around and everybody was pointing the finger at me for holding things up. As far as I was concerned, it was just an inferior backboard. But I sure got the blame for it."

Once the game began, Connors tried to make the crowd forget about the long delay. He played tough defense and scored eight points, but that wasn't enough. Chicago nipped Boston 57–55.

"Hell, it's fun talking about the shattered backboard now, but back then I was looking for a place to hide," said Connors. "Can you imagine what today's Celtics fans would do to you if you delayed one of their precious games like that?"

How did the NBA's all-time worst team score the winning basket to break its twenty-game losing streak?

On a goal-tending call. On their way to establishing the worst record in NBA history, 9–73, the 1972–73 Philadelphia 76ers lost twenty straight games before beating the Milwaukee Bucks 106–104 when Milwaukee center Dick Cunningham was called for goal-tending with sixteen seconds left in the game.

Butch Morgan

Coach ■ College of St. Joseph the Provider ■ December 11, 1974

Talk about poetic injustice. Before a big game, Coach Butch Morgan read his team a poem he hoped would lead the squad to victory. Unfortunately, the verse did just the reverse.

In the locker room—before the St. Joseph cagers of Rutland, Vermont, tangled with their more powerful rival, Castleton State College—Morgan tried to psyche up his players with an inspirational poem called "Don't Quit." He made copies of the ode and gave one to each player before reading it out loud.

"After I read the poem to them, I asked their response to it," recalled Morgan. "I took a few extra minutes to make sure each player had the chance to study the poem and talk about it. The gym was jammed and the fans were waiting for us to come out. The ref kept coming into the locker room telling us to get out on the floor and I kept telling him we weren't done yet. I felt what I was doing in the locker room was more important than what was going to happen on the court, anyway."

The refs found no rhyme or reason for Morgan's muse. When St. Joseph finally came out onto the floor, the officials assessed the team five technical fouls—one for each starting player—for delaying the game. Before the clock ticked off a single second, Castleton's Dave Bove shot five technical free throws and made three of them. They turned out to be crucial points: St. Joseph lost 79–78.

Despite losing because of the poem, Morgan called the game "the high point" of his coaching career. "I expected my team to get beat by fifteen or twenty points, yet those kids played a phenomenal game. In all honesty," added Morgan, who now runs a bar in Rutland, "they probably would have won it—with a little bit of decent coaching."

Wichita State Fans

January 26, 1952

The moment referees Alex George and Cliff Ogden stepped onto the court at the raucous and rowdy Forum in Wichita, they knew they were in for a long, brutal night. But they had no idea just how long and brutal it would be.

The Forum—site of a clash between the Wichita State Shockers and the rival Drake Bulldogs—would have inspired Dante. It was a hellhole for officials and visiting teams. The cramped arena had a balcony that practically hung out over the court, an ideal spot for fans to bombard refs and opposing players with flying objects.

But the worst spectators weren't students—they were cowboys who galloped into the cattle town every Saturday night to kick up some dust. First they hung out at the nearby Cattlemen's Cafe, then they got tanked up and moseyed over to the Forum to help—by hook or by crook—their Shockers rustle up a victory.

During the Drake game, whenever the calls went against Wichita State, troublemaking wranglers in the balcony threw coins at the two officials. The first time referee George went over to pick up one of the coins on the court, he burned his fingers. Only then did he discover that the low-down varmints had toasted the coins with a match before throwing them.

Despite the hoots and hollers and thrown debris, the refs maintained control of a thrilling game. With eight seconds left, Wichita State hit a basket to tie the score at 63–63. Drake called a timeout to set up the final game-winning shot.

When play resumed, Drake worked the ball to its best shooter, who took a shot at the buzzer. "I checked first to see if there was any foul," George recalled. "There wasn't. But when I looked up to watch the flight of the ball, I saw a drunk in the balcony throw his coat over the basket and block the ball from going in.

"The Drake coach was screaming that the shot had to count and the Wichita State coach was yelling that it shouldn't count because the ball wouldn't have gone in the basket anyway.

"I didn't do anything at first because all those damn fans were right on top of us and about to tear the building down. Cliff Ogden [the other official] ran over to me and asked, 'Well, Alex, what are you going to call it?'

"I said, 'How far are we away from our dressing room door?'

"He said, 'About 100 feet.'

" 'The basket has to count, but if I tell them now, we'll never make it out of here with our skins.' We ran to the dressing room door and I turned around and yelled, 'Good!' Then we locked ourselves inside while objects of every kind came flying out from the balcony and a screaming mob covered the court."

After hiding in their dressing room for a couple of hours, the refs gingerly opened the door and scurried outside. The coast was clear—almost. Joe Peters, a friend of George's, carried the ref's bag out to the street, where a little black-haired woman approached them. George had been warned earlier about this woman—she had a reputation for assaulting officials.

Recalled George, "She went up to my friend Joe and said, 'I thought you worked a very fine game.' But before he could tell her that he wasn't the referee, she started beating him over the head with her umbrella. I took action immediately. I told her, 'That's right, he did work a fine game.' After all, Joe had already been hit. There was no sense for me to get beaten up, too!"

Hack Attack

The Foulest Moments of the Syracuse Nationals

• The most fouled-up play-off game ever, March 21, 1953. In wild, brutal quadruple overtime, Nationals and Boston Celtics fight each other and police. Players are whistled for 106 fouls (fifty-five by Syracuse) as twelve (including seven Nationals) foul out. Syracuse loses, 111–105.

• The DQ game, November 15, 1952. Syracuse hatchetmen hack their way to team-high sixty fouls in bloody battle against Baltimore Bullets. So many Nationals foul out—an NBA-record eight—that refs let DQ'ed players back in game so Syracuse can play with five men. Further fouls give Baltimore free throws and technical foul shots. Syracuse loses, 97–91.

• Dick Farley's five-minute assault, March 12, 1956. Guard Dick Farley wastes no time in making presence known by taking just five minutes, an NBA record, to foul out against St. Louis Hawks. Syracuse wins, 97–92.

• The most foul-marred game in NBA history, November 24, 1949. Nationals and Anderson Packers elbow, kick, knee, trip, and slug their way to record 122 personal fouls (fifty-six by Syracuse). All ten starters from both teams foul out. Syracuse wins, 125–123, in five overtimes.

Bill van Breda Kolff

Coach ■ Memphis Tams ■ November 2, 1973

Bill van Breda Kolff earned technicals as if he got commission on them. The coach of the American Basketball Association's Memphis Tams was nailed with four T's in one game! That's a Hall of SHAME

van Breda Kolff giving the ref a new high five   AP/Wide World Photos

feat, considering it takes only two technicals for automatic dismissal from the arena.

"If I had done it right, I could have had five technicals," said van Breda Kolff of his record-setting performance during a game in San Diego.

"Referee Eddie Rush, who would call technicals on me for just looking at him, gave me my first T of the game for jumping up, waving my arms, and protesting a call," the coach recalled. "That made me really angry, so I just got off the bench and went up into the stands and sat with some friends."

But the second official, Jess Kersey, citing an ABA rule that said a coach must remain "in the vicinity" of his team's bench, called another technical on van Breda Kolff and ordered him out of the arena. Fuming mad, the coach refused to leave. Instead, he stalked over to the scorer's table and demanded to look in the rule book. As he thumbed through it, he muttered, "Where does it say where I have to be?"

Then Rush came over and told the timekeeper to set the timeout clock at twenty seconds. "Every twenty seconds that he's still here is another technical," the ref declared.

When twenty seconds passed with van Breda Kolff still flipping through the rule book, he was slapped with his third technical. Recalled the coach, "I still couldn't find the rule in the book, but I told myself, 'This is ridiculous. I could be here forever.' "

Finally, van Breda Kolff left the scorer's table. He started walking off the court just as a San Diego player took the first technical foul shot and missed. The ball caromed directly over to the departing coach. Instead of ignoring the ball or simply tossing it back to the foul line, van Breda Kolff took the ball and, with great dignity, marched across the floor, bowed deeply, and presented it to Rush. Boom! The coach was slapped with T No. 4.

"I didn't play it smart," recounted the coach. "I should have pulled the ball back just as Rush was reaching for it and then kicked the hell out of it. I still have visions of the ball and my loafer flying off the court and me getting my fifth technical."

The technicals cost van Breda Kolff a league fine of $450. "It was worth it," he said.

Andy Landers

Women's Basketball Coach ▪ Georgia ▪ 1974–present

When it comes to coaching tactics, Andy Landers's method ranks at the top for shame.

Whenever he thinks his women's basketball team is playing putrid defense, he announces a stinker of a decree: his players' practice uniforms go unwashed for weeks until he sees better defense.

Several times throughout his twelve-year career, Landers has made the Lady Bulldogs wear dirty, smelly uniforms. Landers, who believes defense is the key to winning, came up with the B.O. M.O. after one particularly frustrating game. "I told the team, 'Hey, our defense stinks. As long as it stinks, we're going to stink, too. Until you start playing defense the way it is meant to be played, we're not going to wash any of your practice stuff.' That caught their attention. It's worked every time since.

"When they pull on that rancid uniform every day, they're reminded why they stink so bad. If they don't come out and give me a better effort defensively, they'll just keep smelling badly."

The last time Landers dropped his stink bomb announcement was in 1986. Even though the Lady Bulldogs were 15–1 and second in the nation at the time, Landers was disgusted with their defensive performance. So he banned the washing of their practice uniforms for nearly three weeks. On the advice of the team trainer, however, the players' socks were exempt from the laundry ban.

Lady Bulldogs getting a whiff of their offensive duds   *Sports Illustrated/Bill Luster*

"We've been stinking it up pretty good, in more ways than one," Landers told the press after the togs had accumulated two weeks' worth of sweat and foul odor. After seeing some improvement during practice, he declared, "If we can play a few games like we've been practicing, we'll throw those babies in the washing machine."

A week later, just when the EPA should have cited the team for violating the Clean Air Act, the uniforms were sent to the laundry. The players could finally breathe a little easier. They lost only one more game the rest of the year and finished second in the nation with a sweet-smelling record of 30–2.

Fred Brown

Guard ■ Georgetown Hoyas ■ March 29, 1982

In all of collegiate national championship action, no blunder remains so etched in fans' minds as the shockingly errant pass made by Fred Brown of the Georgetown Hoyas.

With eight seconds left in the 1982 championship clash, the Hoyas had the ball, but the North Carolina Tar Heels had the lead, 63–62. Brown, the usually reliable guard, rushed the ball upcourt, determined to get it to one of his teammates for the final game-winning basket.

He saw that Sleepy Floyd was covered, as were Patrick Ewing and Ed Spriggs. "I should have called timeout, but I decided to pass it to Eric Smith, who was on the right side of the lane," Brown recalled. "I thought I saw Smitty out of the right corner of my eye. But it wasn't him."

No, it was North Carolina's James Worthy. Brown fired a perfect chest-high pass right into the hands of a happily surprised Worthy, who clutched the ball and then dribbled the other way until he was deliberately fouled with two seconds left. Worthy missed both free throws, but it didn't matter. Georgetown lost 63–62.

"Worthy didn't steal it—I gave it away," said Brown. "My peripheral vision is pretty good, but this time it failed me. It was only a split second. But that's all it takes to lose a game. I knew it was bad as soon as I let it go. If I'd had a rubber band, I would have yanked it back in."

Larry Bird   Julius Erving

Forward ▪ Boston Celtics   Forward ▪ Philadelphia 76ers
November 9, 1984

It was the NBA's version of *Star Wars*. Two of the league's most celebrated players were thrown out of a game for fighting—with each other, no less.

Fans wondered if nothing was sacred after superstars Larry Bird and Julius Erving tried to play one-on-one with their fists. What was so shocking was that Larry and Dr. J were friends and had appeared together on commercials for sneakers and a computer game. Yet the two storied players showed that neither man would give an inch, regardless of their personal and professional relationship off the court.

Erving, of the Philadelphia 76ers, was matched up against Bird and the Boston Celtics in an emotional, tense, early-season battle between the two unbeaten teams at the Boston Garden. It turned into a rough, frustrating game for Dr. J, who suffered a rare off-night. By late in the third quarter, the All-Star Philly forward had scored only eight points while Larry, the NBA's MVP, had hit seventeen of twenty-three shots and rolled up forty-two points. No one would have blamed the good doctor for walking off the court and looking for a quiet place to practice in the Berkshires.

Throughout the game (won by Boston, 130–119), Bird and Erving kept pushing and shoving each other. With 1:38 left in the third period and the Celtics ahead 95–75, things turned ugly. Bird had the ball and tried to shake off Erving, whose hands were all over him. But Bird was whistled for an offensive foul for throwing an elbow at Erving. As the two stars trotted back upcourt, they traded insults with each other. They were jaw-to-jaw when suddenly Erving grabbed Bird's neck and Larry retaliated by clutching Dr. J by the throat.

Bird threw a couple of punches before he was collared by Sixers center Moses Malone, who got Bird in a headlock. Then Philly's Charles Barkley came up from behind and pinned both of Bird's arms. While Larry was being held back, Erving landed three quick right-handed jabs at Bird, who finally worked free from Barkley's grasp. Meanwhile, both benches had cleared and several fights had broken out. After order was restored, Bird was still so irate that he attempted to break away from his teammates' restraint to get at Erving.

Erving and Bird playing one-on-one   AP/Wide World Photos

Since brawling has no place on a basketball court, referee Dick Bavetta did what fans and players alike had thought could never happen—he gave Bird and Erving the old heave-ho. It was the first and only time Dr. J had been thrown out of a game in his entire distinguished career. The ejection was also rare for Bird, who has seldom lost his cool.

Bird and Erving were each fined $7,500 by the league, which levied another $15,500 on the sixteen others involved in the melee started by the two superstars—superstars who should have stuck to making baskets instead of making war.

Kevin Doherty

Guard ■ Davidson College ■ January 5, 1976

Some college basketball players have gone through an entire four years of school without earning any recognition. Kevin Doherty gained notoriety in just thirty-eight seconds. That's how long it took him to rack up *four* personal fouls.

Midway in the second half, the second-string sophomore guard for the Davidson College Wildcats was sitting on the bench watching the visiting University of Virginia Cavaliers pull steadily away from his team. Suddenly, Davidson coach Bo Brickels summoned Doherty and said, "Get in there and make something happen."

The coach was thinking along the lines of inspired play. What he saw instead was foul play.

Just two seconds after Doherty first touched the ball, while bringing it up the court, he was called for charging. Then, on defense, he picked up his second personal foul just fourteen seconds later. Seventeen seconds after that, he hacked Virginia's Billy Langloh on the arm for his third foul. A few seconds later, Langloh stole the ball from Doherty, went in for a layup—and paid the price as Doherty shoved him against the basketball standards. Only thirty-eight seconds had ticked off the clock and already Doherty had tallied four personal fouls—an amazing record for swiftness (although the NCAA doesn't officially keep track of such things).

"Kevin fouled guys so fast that no one realized what had happened," recalled Brickels. Doherty finally managed to contain himself for over four minutes before committing his fifth foul. He was whistled to the bench just 5:06 after he had entered the game.

"It was a night to remember," recalled Doherty, "or was it a night to forget?" In a classic bit of understatement, he added, "In that game, I may have been a mite too aggressive."

Uncharitable Stripe

The charity stripe was anything but kind to Wilt "The Stilt" Chamberlain.

Even though he was the only player in NBA history ever to score one hundred points in a single game, Chamberlain was one of the sorriest foul shooters in the league.

Wilt—who played for the Warriors in Philadelphia and San Francisco, the Philadelphia 76ers, and the Los Angeles Lakers—set several dubious marks at the foul line that he would like to forget:

- most foul shots missed in a game—22
- most foul shots missed in a season—528
- most foul shots missed in a play-off game—17

University of California at Santa Cruz Sea Lions

January 8, 1982

If the Indians at Little Big Horn had played basketball for the University of California at Santa Cruz, Custer's Last Stand would never have happened.

The Cal-Santa Cruz Sea Lions played in a foul-plagued game that depleted the opposing team until it was down to one player on the court. Yet five Sea Lions still couldn't overtake the "team" of one. They couldn't stop him from scoring five points on his own in the final two minutes and saving the game for his school.

Cal-Santa Cruz was trailing the West Coast Christian College Knights by fifteen points midway through the second half when the Knights got into serious foul trouble. Because of injuries, the team only suited up eight players—too few in a game officiated by two whistle-happy refs. When the fourth Knight fouled out, the Sea Lions had a five-man-to-four-man advantage, but still couldn't narrow the lead—even when more West Coast Christian players fouled out. The Knights continued to draw more whistles than Loni Anderson at a hard-hat convention until, finally, with 2:10 left to play, West Coast Christian was down to its last player: Mike Lockhart, a 6-foot, 1-inch junior guard. According to the rules, a game can continue when a team has only one player left if that team is leading or has a chance to win.

Lockhart's coach, Jerry Turner, called time out and conferred with the officials. Turner then explained to Lockhart that the guard could inbound the ball only by having it touched by an opposing player. The coach's final words to him were, "Don't foul."

A foul would have ended the game because Lockhart had four personals and there was no one left to replace him. The Sea Lions, with a squad of nine, were in much better shape even though four of their starters had fouled out.

"We had started in a straight 2–3 zone," Lockhart recalled. "After we were down to four guys, we used a 2–2 box. Then a 1–2 diamond. Then a 1–1 zone. Finally a 1."

When Lockhart found himself alone on the floor, West Coast Christian was ahead 70–57. "I was scared to death," he said. "I had confidence in my ball handling, but I had four fouls myself and there

17

was nobody to pass to. The coach told me to calm down and take my time."

If ever the Sea Lions were going to close the thirteen-point gap, it would be in these final two minutes when they played five-on-one basketball. But since they had never practiced any plays for this situation, they acted like they didn't know what to do. One player was called for traveling on a layup and another got whistled for a three-second lane violation. "Nothing seemed to go right for them," recalled Turner. "Their players were fighting over the shots. It was chaos."

Said Cal-Santa Cruz coach Joe Richardson, "On offense, we tried planting a player under our basket and heaving the ball downcourt to him, but the pass went wild. We also tried working it down with shorter passes. But in the excitement, another pass went out of bounds."

Meanwhile, Lockhart did what he could. He rolled the ball in bounds, jogging alongside and waiting for an opponent to touch it so he could snatch it back. He retrieved another inbounds pass by bouncing the ball off the leg of an opponent. The Sea Lions were so inept that they let Lockhart grab a rebound from them. He even blocked one shot against a player who was five inches taller than he was—and nearly gave his coach heart failure. "I was afraid he might have been called for a foul on the play," said Turner, who shouted to Lockhart to lay off the shot-blocking routine.

When he got possession of the ball, Lockhart managed to eat up time by weaving his way through the Cal-Santa Cruz defenses until he was fouled. He made five of six free throws.

"Our biggest mistake was fouling him," said Richardson. "It was just unintelligent on our part. But I suppose my players became frustrated when they couldn't get the ball from him."

Despite their four-man advantage, the Sea Lions scored only ten points and gave up five—not nearly enough to overcome the thirteen-point deficit. They lost 75–67.

Sacramento Kings

February 4, 1987

In the worst first-quarter performance in pro basketball history, the Sacramento Kings missed every single shot from the floor.

Playing in the Forum against the first-place Los Angeles Lakers, the last-place Kings looked like they had all flunked Basket Weaving 101—they couldn't make a basket in eighteen tries in the opening period. No jams, no jumpers, no sky hooks, no tip-ins, no three-point bombs, no nothing.

After the first twelve minutes, the scoreboard read Lakers 40, Kings 4. Sacramento had scored fewer points in the first quarter than any team since the introduction of the twenty-four-second clock in 1954.

Kings coach Phil Johnson called a timeout 2:11 into the game, after the Lakers jumped out to a 10–0 lead. Two minutes later, Chick Hearn, the Lakers' announcer, set a record for the earliest prediction of an NBA victory when he told his listeners, "This game is in the refrigerator." The score was 16–0 and Johnson had called his second timeout to regroup his troops. It didn't help. The beleaguered coach was forced to use his third timeout at 5:26 after Los Angeles guard Byron Scott's breakaway jam made it 22–0.

Sacramento had fallen behind by an unbelievable 29–0 score when the Kings' Derek Smith was fouled with 2:54 left in the period. The pressure was on. Could he do what no one else on his team could do—put the ball through the hoop? Eyeing the basket as if this were a possible game-winning foul shot, Smith took a deep breath and tossed the ball through the basket for Sacramento's first point. The Laker crowd went wild and gave Smith a standing ovation.

The Kings' entire offense in the opening period came from the charity line where they managed to sink four foul shots. The quarter ended with the Lakers leading by ten times Sacramento's tally, 40–4.

Not until their twenty-second field goal attempt, when Eddie Johnson banked in a three-footer twenty seconds into the second period, did the Kings experience the joy of making a two-pointer. After breaking the ice, Sacramento played L.A. even the rest of the way and lost 128–92.

"In the eighth grade something like this happened to me," said Derek Smith. "We scored like fourteen points, and the other guys had eighty. I remember I cried for a few days after that. You can't do that here. But the Lakers toyed with us like we were little kids.

"When you're down 10–0 to the Lakers, you know it's getting bad. When it's 16–0, you know it's real bad. When it's 22–0, you're critical, and they might as well pull the plug."

Oklahoma Sooners   Missouri Tigers

Women's Basketball Teams ■ January 17, 1987

Women basketball players may smell better and look prettier on the court than their male counterparts, but the gals can duke it out with just as much toughness as the guys.

The Oklahoma Sooners and Missouri Tigers proved that basket-brawling is not for men only when the women players tangled in a cat fight that could have earned them scholarships in roller derby or mud wrestling. For five wild minutes, they punched, kicked, and clawed each other on the court immediately after Mizzou's 72–70 home-court victory.

The fuse was lit with twenty-four seconds left in the game when Oklahoma's Margaret McKeon fouled Lisa Ellis. Ellis took exception to the hacking and showed her displeasure by bounce-passing the ball off McKeon's face. The refs didn't think that was very ladylike and slapped Ellis with a technical foul.

Sooners and Tigers banging the (floor)boards   Jim Noelker/*Columbia Tribune* Photo

Despite the incident, the two teams still went through with the postgame handshaking ritual—until it was interrupted by Sooner coach Maura McHugh, who confronted Ellis. When the volatile coach shook a finger in Ellis's face, Ellis angrily pushed McHugh's hand away. Oklahoma's Lisa Allison then grabbed Ellis from behind and that signaled the start of the free-for-all.

While some players were trading in-your-face jams without the ball, others were rolling around on the floor, kicking and punching each other. Ellis got the worst of it and sustained a broken nose and bruised ribs. McHugh was body-slammed to the hardwood where she kept kicking the Tigers while she was on her back. "I was punched in the back of the head and kicked in the ribs," she told the press. "When I was on the floor, I was hit more times than anyone. If I didn't kick, I'd still be down there. It was just a matter of survival."

After a brief investigation, the University of Missouri announced that two members of the team had been suspended for one game each because of their "retaliatory action."

When asked if she had tried to make peace with McHugh, Missouri coach Joann Rutherford said, "I always try to shake the opposing coach's hand, but how could I when she was on the floor?"

Terry Holland

Coach ■ University of Virginia ■ 1977

Coach Terry Holland got so caught up in teaching his players how to dunk a basketball that he nearly hanged himself—literally.

At practice one day, Holland decided his University of Virginia squad could use a lesson in basketball's most spectacular shot. He got the idea after noticing that one of the hydraulic baskets in the gym was a little bit lower than it should have been. "It wasn't all that noticeable but the basket was low enough so an old-timer like me could still dunk the ball easily," recalled Holland, a former star at Davidson. "I put together some really impressive dunks on this particular basket.

"I called over to one of my players who was 6 feet, 4 inches tall but not a very good jumper. I thought I would open his eyes a little bit so I told him, 'Watch me, because I'm going to show you how to make a good baseline move.'

"I drove the baseline, came back under the basket, and dunked the ball behind my head. As I did this, my whistle popped out of my shirt, went up and over the basket, and wrapped itself around the rim.

"I hate to admit this, but I almost hanged myself. Fortunately, with my momentum, the string on my whistle broke, or else I would have been left dangling. I still received a pretty good jerk. It surprised the hell out of me and it put me down on the seat of my pants.

"I was sitting there on the floor, rubbing my neck and wondering what happened when the kid came up to me and said, 'Are you sure that's the way you want me to dunk, coach?' "

Joe Soskovic

Referee ■ February 12, 1978

Referee Joe Soskovic was such a stickler for the rules that he called a technical foul for overexuberance—after the game was over.

Because of his uncalled-for call, the Southern Connecticut State Owls' apparent 70–69 victory turned into a totally unfair 2–0 forfeit defeat.

The 8–10 Owls were beating the highly favored 13–5 Springfield College Chiefs 70–69 with five seconds left in the game when Southern Connecticut's Daryl Breland stole the ball at midcourt. He dribbled toward his basket until time ran out and the buzzer sounded.

To celebrate his team's upset victory, Breland tried to slam dunk the ball. Unfortunately, Breland did it right in front of Soskovic, who believed that this typical collegiate response to a hard-fought win was a blatant violation of the rules. So, even though time had expired and the coaches were shaking each other's hands, Soskovic called a technical foul on Breland.

Soskovic claimed the game is not over until the referee approves the final score with the official scorer. Since Breland dunked the ball before the final score was approved, Soskovic ruled that the player had committed a violation—dunking a dead ball. For this heinous crime, Springfield's Don Lemieux was allowed a technical foul shot which he made to tie the score at 70–all and send the game into overtime.

But Southern Connecticut coach Ed Brown, furious at Soskovic, declared that his team had won fair and square. The rightfully angered coach refused to put his team back on the floor. "As far as I'm concerned, we won the game," Brown said later. "With all due conscience, I couldn't continue to play. So I told my kids, 'Let's go. The game is over.' Then we started running off the floor." Soskovic responded by awarding Springfield a 2–0 forfeit victory.

The ref didn't have to worry about getting booed off the court because the game was played at Springfield's Memorial Field House. He also had some further support when, during all the fuss, he conferred with Dr. Edward Steitz, the editor of the rule book of the International Association of Approved Basketball Officials—who just happened to be the athletic director of Springfield College. "As far as I'm concerned, the official called it by the book," said Steitz.

The Owls filed a formal protest but the Eastern College Athletic Conference disallowed it, claiming "technically, the official's call was correct."

Since the arbiters were so stuck on technicalities, they should have ruled in favor of Southern Connecticut—because technically Breland didn't dunk the ball. He missed the basket! "It wasn't a dunk because he never reached the rim," said coach Brown. "The ball never went into the basket."

Whether or not Breland took the ball and dunked it, Soskovic should have taken his call and stuffed it.

Milking It for All It's Worth

For helping them win the 1961 Western Athletic Conference championship, the University of Utah Runnin' Redskins (now called Utes) honored their coach, Jack Gardner, by pulling off a nasty joke. Minutes before their final regular season game, the players gave Gardner a big bottle of milk. The coach thanked them because he was a compulsive milk drinker who guzzled the stuff during games in the belief that it helped calm his nervous stomach. But he didn't learn—until it was too late—that his players had added some milk of magnesia to the bottle. That night, Gardner became a full-fledged Runnin' Redskin.

Randy Smith

Guard ■ Buffalo Braves ■ 1973

As a young guard for the NBA's Buffalo Braves, Randy Smith learned how to play tough defense and run the offense. However, he never quite learned how to call timeouts.

"He used to do things you wouldn't believe," said Jack Ramsay, then coach of the Braves. Although Smith became a two-time All-Star and averaged 17.4 points per game in ten seasons, he used to give Ramsay fits playing for the lowly expansion team early in his career.

Recalling a game against the Milwaukee Bucks, Ramsay said, "The Bucks ran off six straight points, so I wanted a timeout. Randy was bringing the ball up and I yelled, 'Randy, timeout!' He just left the ball in the middle of his dribble and came over. He forgot to call it."

Randy pulled another dandy later that same year during a game against the Golden State Warriors in San Francisco where the Braves were trying to break a seven-game losing streak. That night, Buffalo played exceptionally well and, thanks to Smith's thirteen points in the third quarter, took a 79–67 lead into the fourth period.

But the Warriors launched a furious rally and closed the margin to within a basket, 99–97, in the final minute. Then Golden State covered the Braves with a full-court press, as Randy tried to find an open teammate. With the clock ticking down and the crowd screaming, Coach Ramsay yelled at Smith to call a timeout.

Now how hard could that be? All Randy had to do was (1) hold on to the ball, (2) turn to the ref, (3) say, "Timeout," (4) wait for the official to award the timeout, and (5) flip him the ball. Incredibly, Smith skipped steps 1, 3, and 4. At a crucial moment when the game was on the line, Randy casually turned to referee Mendy Rudolph and tossed him the ball without ever calling time. Rudolph quickly jumped out of the way. The loose ball was picked up by Jeff Mullins of the Warriors, who promptly drove in for a layup to tie the score.

Without giving Smith another chance to goof up, Buffalo's Bob McAdoo called for—and got—a timeout. "I was beside myself," coach Ramsay recalled. "I said, 'Randy, what are you doing?' He looked puzzled and said, 'Coach, the ref *knew* I was throwing it to him.'" The Braves never recovered from Smith's blunder. They went on to lose their eighth straight, 106–101.

Who took the most shameful trip ever to the free-throw line?

Elmore Smith. In a game on December 28, 1974, the Los Angeles Lakers' center went to the line with a three-to-make-two situation. Not one of his shots ever touched the rim, the backboard, or the net. He had tossed up *three* air balls.

THE GOLF HALL OF SHAME

Lee Trevino

British Open ■ July 12, 1970

St. Andrews is the birthplace of golf—and the site of Lee Trevino's biggest blunder.

Going into the final round of the 1970 British Open, Super Mex had a total of 207 and held a three-stroke edge over Jack Nicklaus, Doug Sanders, and Tony Jacklin, all tied for second at 210.

But Trevino slipped badly and quickly lost his lead. What finally beat him was the colossal boner he pulled on the fifth hole. The distinctive feature of the hole is its huge, unusual double green that has two cups for two separate holes. Even though Trevino had played the fifth hole three times in the tournament, his usual alertness faded like a sliced drive.

Pulling an iron out of his bag for an approach shot, Lee studied the green and sent the ball straight for the flag—the wrong flag. The ball landed 80 feet away from the right hole. The moment he hit the approach shot, Trevino slapped himself on the forehead, like one of the Three Stooges, and said, "I done hit to the wrong stick!" Then he added, "And I'm just dumb enough to have done it, too."

He three-putted for a bogey at a time when Nicklaus and Sanders were pulling away from the pack. Lee never recovered from his goof and wound up watching Nicklaus win the British Open in a play-off against Sanders.

Trevino: "I done hit to the wrong stick!"   UPI/Bettmann Newsphotos

Bobby Cruickshank

U.S. Open ■ June 9, 1934

Bobby Cruickshank lost the 1934 U.S. Open when he threw his club—not in anger, but in joy.

Leading at the turn by two strokes in the final round at the Merion Country Club near Philadelphia, the small, wiry Scot was hoping to hold his lead with a par four on the 378-yard eleventh hole. After hitting a decent drive off the tee, he swatted a weak approach shot. To his dismay, the ball fell into the creek running in front of the green, and the gallery groaned as the shot sent up a huge splash of water. But suddenly the crowd broke into wild cheers as the ball bounced out of the water and up onto the green ten feet away from the pin. The ball had been saved from a watery grave by sheer luck—it had hit the only submerged flat rock in the stream.

Bobby was so elated that he tossed his club exuberantly into the air, tipped his cap, and shouted, "Thank you, God!" While he continued to celebrate, he failed to notice that his club was now descending—until it conked him on the noggin and knocked him to the ground! He saw more birdies than he made during the tournament.

The dazed golfer managed to get back on his feet and two-putted for a par. But Cruickshank never fully recovered from the shock and pain of being clubbed by his own club. Only twice on the next seven holes was he able to make par as he tumbled from first place to a third-place finish.

Cruickshank seeing nothing but birdies   AP/Wide World Photos

Ray Ainsley

Ray Ainsley holds the record for the most incredible score in the U.S. Open. He shot a nineteen—on one hole!

And from that moment on, Ainsley has been the patron saint of duffers the world over.

Ray carded a triple-triple-triple-triple-triple bogey on the par four sixteenth hole at Cherry Hills Country Club in Denver during the second round of the 1938 championship. The young Californian, playing in his first Open, had been shooting respectable golf, although he was never in contention. He would have been just another name in a long list of qualifiers if he hadn't swung his way to shame on one hole.

Ainsley immediately found himself in trouble when he hooked his drive into the rough. That set him up for a disastrous second shot which dropped into a shallow, but swift-moving creek running in front of the green. Ray looked over the situation—the ball was on a sand bar a few inches under the clear, cold water—and decided he had a playable lie. Playable for a trout, maybe, but not a golfer.

Nevertheless, Ainsley took off his shoes and socks, drew a blaster out of his bag, and planted his feet in the creek. Just as he went into his swing, the current moved the ball downstream a few inches. He hit nothing but water and sand. So he took a new stance and swung again . . . and again . . . and again. Ray missed each time as the current pushed the ball farther and farther away from him. Leaping about the creek and flailing away at the water with his iron, Ainsley was soaked and splattered with sand, but he refused to give up.

On the bank, Ray's playing partner, Bud McKinney, had jammed his fist into his mouth to keep from laughing. But official scorer Red Anderson, who was calling the strokes out loud, couldn't contain himself after the count reached nine. Falling on the ground in stitches, Anderson told McKinney between guffaws, "Take over the count, Bud."

So McKinney dutifully shouted, "Ten! . . . Eleven! . . . Twelve! . . ."

Finally, on his thirteenth stroke, Ainsley nailed the ball. It soared out of the water like a Polaris missile—a misguided one. The ball crashed into a clump of bushes well beyond the green. The never-say-die Ray worked his way through the brush and found his ball. It took him *three* more whacks before the ball plopped onto the green. Then, as if a sixth sense told him that he could break the old record of eighteen, Ainsley three-putted. The record was his—the worst score ever for one hole in a pro championship.

"And everybody loved him for it," wrote Chester Nelson, sports editor of *The Rocky Mountain News*, who was covering the tournament. Nelson said Ray's dubious achievement was applauded by "all the dubs [boneheads] who ever forgot to touch second base, all the dubs who ever ran backwards in the last quarter, and all the other dubs."

Skulled Shot

Bobby Cruickshank wasn't the only pro to literally skull a shot. It happened to Ben Crenshaw, too.

During the PGA championship in Toledo on August 9, 1986, Crenshaw tossed his nine iron into the air when his approach shot almost went into the cup on the eighteenth hole. The club spun around twice, and as Crenshaw reached out to catch it, the flange hit the back of his head, opening a small gash.

Crenshaw, embarrassed and bleeding, two-putted for par and then was hustled off to Toledo Hospital where he received three stitches to close the wound.

The incident prompted golf wags to observe that, while hackers often skull their wedges, it's rare that a pro wedges his skull.

Andy Bean

Canadian Open ■ July 30, 1983

Andy Bean made an easy two-inch tap-in at the 1983 Canadian Open—yet it cost him a chance to win.

During the third round, Bean's ball was resting two inches from the cup on the fifteenth green. Being lazy, cute or absent-minded, Bean tapped the ball in with the *grip* of his putter instead of the head.

A PGA Tour official who saw the stroke on television noticed that Bean had committed an infraction. Bean didn't know he had violated Rule 19 which states: "The ball shall be fairly struck at with the head of the club and must not be pushed, scraped or spooned." When word reached him, Bean had to change his score to reflect the two-stroke penalty that was assessed against him.

Although he was irritated with himself, Bean didn't think much of the gaffe because at the time of the incident he seemed out of contention. But the final round became bittersweet for him when he shot a record-tying sixty-two and finished the tournament with a five-under-par total of 279. For nearly three hours, Bean, an early starter, waited in the clubhouse to see if his score would hold up. Unfortunately, he missed getting into a play-off by just two strokes— the measure of his penalty.

"What can I say?" Bean told reporters afterward. "It was a dumb-ass thing to do."

Tommy Aaron

The Masters ■ April 14, 1968

During the 1968 Masters, Tommy Aaron had little problem with his woods, irons, and putter. Where he was weakest was in handling the pencil—because Tommy made the biggest scorecard blunder in golfing history.

According to the rules of professional golf, a player is responsible for the accuracy of his scorecard even though he does not keep his own score; his playing partner does. Each player checks his score, then both sign the card, attesting to its correctness. The rule reads "If the competitor returns a score for any hole lower than actually played, he shall be disqualified. A score higher than actually played must stand as returned."

Because of this rule, Aaron deprived playing partner Roberto de Vicenzo of at least a tie and perhaps a victory in golf's most prestigious tournament—the Masters in Augusta, Georgia. De Vicenzo was playing brilliant golf and was tied for first on the seventeenth hole of the final round. In full view of the gallery and countless millions of TV watchers, Roberto scored a birdie three.

But Aaron carelessly marked him down for a par four. De Vicenzo finished the tournament with a remarkable score of 277, eleven under par. Before signing and handing over Roberto's scorecard, Aaron compounded his error by marking the back nine holes with a total of thirty-five instead of thirty-four and the overall total of sixty-six instead of sixty-five. Anxious to see the finish of co-leader Bob Goalby, who was still out on the course, the tired de Vicenzo gave his scorecard a cursory glance and signed it, having complete faith in Aaron's scorekeeping ability.

Masters officials then marched Roberto to the clubhouse to prepare for a TV interview. Minutes later, they called him back—and informed him that his card was inaccurate. The four that Aaron had written on de Vicenzo's scorecard stood as official, giving Roberto a 278 instead of a 277. When Goalby came in later with a 277, he was declared the winner.

Aaron's goof, and de Vicenzo's failure to catch it, cost Roberto the chance to win the $20,000 first prize and collect an estimated $1 million in promotional fees. Said Roberto afterward, "Tommy feels like I feel—very bad."

Card Blanch

Signing incorrect scorecards has happened to the best of pros. But at least they learned their lesson.

Ladies' pro Colleen Walker apparently flunked her course on scorecard signing. Not once, but *twice* in 1986, Colleen wrote her moniker on incorrect cards. In Toronto, the mistake cost her a piddling $2,500 paycheck. However, in New York's MasterCard International, her gaffe cost her $18,500—and a second-place finish.

Gary Player

Huddersfield, England ■ June 12, 1955

In one of the most shameful shots in golf history, Gary Player was knocked out by his own ball.

Making his first trip to England, the young South African pro was battling for the lead in a tournament in Huddersfield. As he teed up for the final hole, he needed a par four to win and a bogey to tie.

After Player hooked his drive in the rough, his second shot landed to the right of the green only inches away from a stone wall. There wasn't enough room for his backswing to chip onto the green, and Gary didn't want to waste a shot by tapping the ball clear of the wall before chipping.

That's when he came up with what he figured was a brilliant idea—he'd bounce the ball off the wall. Like a pool player planning a bank shot off the cushion, Gary determined the exact spot where the ball should ricochet to the green.

"I tried to be fancy," wrote Player years ago. "The ball came off the wall in fine shape, but instead of finishing on the green, it ricocheted back and hit me on the cheek. The force of the blow actually knocked me cold momentarily.

"Finally, I regained my senses, at least a portion of them. Still groggy, I chipped onto the green and then somehow knocked the long putt into the hole."

Gary gave a sigh of relief, believing that he had tied for the lead and would be in a play-off. But a tourney official had the unpleasant task of informing Player that he had incurred a two-stroke penalty for impeding the flight of the ball because it had struck him. Thus, Gary lost the tournament by taking it on the chin.

Gerald Ford

Ex-President ▪ United States of America ▪ January 29, 1981

Gerald Ford stated for the record in 1984, "I deny allegations by Bob Hope . . . that during my last game I hit an eagle, a birdie, an elk, and a moose."

Okay, so the former President didn't hit an eagle or a birdie, he's still a golf nut who appears regularly on the pro-am circuit—where his temper is sometimes as short as his putts.

It's par for the course for Ford to be so obstinate that he simply refuses to take an unplayable lie. Instead, he will hopelessly and angrily flail away at the ball while those around him nearly bust a gut to keep from laughing.

This was never more true than when Jerry played in a pro-am at famed Pebble Beach in 1981. Playing with the likes of Arnold Palmer and Hale Irwin, Ford was determined to hold his own. However, his tee shot on the par four, 327-yard fourth hole sailed onto the beach, resting on the surf-pounded rocks. Rather than take a two-stroke penalty and play a new ball, he hiked down to the rocky beach to hit his old ball.

"He was absolutely determined to the point of bullheadedness," recalled Moose Wammock, the former PGA official who handled Ford's security in tour pro-ams. "The ball has to be at rest before you can hit it, and that was what was so funny. About the time he would get set and go into his swing, in came the surf and there went the ball. The ocean kept moving the ball and Jerry kept hacking away. The more he hacked, the madder he got. All you could see was a big spray of water and sand whenever he swung and missed. The only thing you could hear above the sound of the ocean was Jerry swearing."

Eventually, Ford managed to smack the ball back onto the fairway. But then, just when it looked like his troubles were over, he overshot the green! He ended up with a thirteen.

"You can always tell how Jerry is doing by watching the Secret Service," said Wammock. "If the agents are walking close to him, it means he's playing great golf. If they're as far away as allowed, then you know he's playing badly and doesn't want anyone near him.

"The funniest thing about Jerry is not his temper. It's his clumsiness," Wammock claimed. "I guarantee you that there's not a tee marker on a course that he has played on that he hasn't fallen over. It's automatic. He trips over a tee marker every time he plays."

PFC Eddie Martin

Caddy ■ U.S. Open ■ June 15, 1946

Golfing great Bobby Jones once said, "No one ever wins the U.S. Open—someone always loses it."

Caddy Eddie Martin proved those sage words when he unwittingly lost the 1946 Open for Byron Nelson.

Shortly before the tournament, Martin, Nelson's regular caddy, had joined the army and was a PFC stationed in Panama that spring. Yet he was so eager to tote Lord Byron's bag in the Open that Martin managed to get a furlough and arrived in time for the tourney at Canterbury Golf Club in Cleveland. Clad in his GI duds, Martin cheerfully lugged Nelson's clubs and rooted harder than ever for his golfing boss. Yet the caddy cost Nelson the championship.

It happened on the sixteenth hole in the third round after Nelson sliced his drive into the gallery. Wanting to make sure no one

Another missed putt par for the course   AP/Wide World Photos

would accidentally step on the ball, Martin bulled his way through the mob, ducked under the guarding rope, and dutifully pushed aside the surging crowd. In his haste to protect Nelson's ball, the caddy didn't see it until he was right on top of it. But by then it was too late. He unintentionally kicked the ball with his army boot—leaving tournament officials no choice but to assess Nelson a penalty stroke. Martin, who nearly burst into tears, was comforted by Nelson, who absolved him of all blame. But the golfer couldn't overcome the extra stroke.

A score of 283 would have won the championship outright. But because of that extra penalty stroke, Nelson finished with a total of 284 and was forced into a play-off, which he lost to Lloyd Mangrum. The only thing Martin had left to kick after that was himself.

Hale Irwin

British Open ■ July 16, 1983

Hale Irwin made the most pitiful putt in pro golf—and it cost him the 1983 British Open.

"Everyone has an embarrassing moment and this one is mine," said Irwin as he recalled the "air ball" he made on the fourteenth green during the third round.

Irwin's ball was resting just a measly three inches away from the cup. It was a sure par, a gimmee for weekend golfers. Irwin decided to tap it in with a casual backhand stroke of his two-sided putter just as he had done hundreds of times before. But incredibly, when he took his short, easy swing, the putter hit the ground behind the ball and bounced right over it. The putter never touched the ball.

"It was one of those times when I just went into a momentary coma," Irwin said. "Certainly it was as much a shock to everyone else as it was to me. I had to count it as a stroke because there was intent to hit the ball.

"Nobody would have remembered my air ball if it hadn't been for Tom Watson." Irwin finished his final round only one stroke behind Watson, who was still playing. As Watson approached the eighteenth green, needing two putts to par and win the British Open, Irwin was praying for a miracle. Not that Watson would three-putt; rather that he would one-putt.

"I was hoping Tom would win it by two strokes so my little air ball wouldn't have meant much," said Irwin. "Wouldn't you know that he two-putted the eighteenth to win by just one stroke.

Hail, Hale, king of the air ball!   UPI/Bettmann Newsphotos

"I learned never to take anything for granted or play carelessly. That was probably the most expensive—and embarrassing—putting lesson in history. At least it was for me."

What pro golfer was disqualified from two tournaments because he failed to recognize his own ball?

Wayne Grady. On January 26, 1986, during the Phoenix Open, Grady played someone else's ball and was DQ'ed. Then, a month later, at the Los Angeles Open, he got deeked again for playing another wrong ball. True, they were both round and white, but . . .

Putting on the Fritz

Disasters on the Green

• Shortest missed putt on the seventy-second hole to lose the U.S. Open by one stroke—three feet, by Bob Rosburg, 1969.

• Shortest whiffed putt to lose the British Open by one stroke—one inch, on the fourteenth hole, by Andrew Kirkaldy, 1889. After his one-handed stab failed to touch the ball, Kirkaldy said, "If the hole were big enough, I'd bury myself in it."

• Shortest missed putt to lose the U.S. Open—six inches, by Harry Vardon, 1913. As a result of his carelessness, he finished in a three-way tie and lost the play-off.

• Most putts ever needed to sink an easy three-footer in a major tournament—twelve, by Brian Barnes, 1968 French Open. After blowing an easy one-yard putt for par, the British pro tried to rake the ball back into the cup—and missed. So did his next putt and the one after that. Livid with rage, Barnes began batting the ball back and forth, once straddling the line of his putt for a two-stroke penalty. He finally holed out for a fifteen.

T.C. Chen

U.S. Open ■ June 16, 1985

T.C. Chen double-marched his way to golfing shame in the 1985 U.S. Open. He hit his ball twice on one swing—an oh-no no-no that cost him the championship.

The 26-year-old Taiwanese touring pro had led the world's best golfers after each of the first three rounds at Oakland Hills Country Club in Birmingham, Michigan. Ahead by four strokes entering the par four fifth hole in the final round, T.C. suddenly found the going N.G. After a fine drive, he sliced his second shot into the rough and pushed his third into even taller grass about twenty yards from the pin.

For his fourth shot, Chen chose a sand wedge that he normally used for bunker shots. He swung softly, causing his club to snag for a split second in the heavy grass. But that was all it took for T.C. to turn a typical swing into one of golf's most infamous shots. Incredibly, as the ball hung in the air, it was struck again, this time by the follow-through of the clubface. Striking the ball twice on the same swing is an infraction of the rules that calls for a penalty stroke. Chen stood frozen in shock. He had never seen a double-hit—let alone made one. And of all the times for it to happen, he had to make this rare blunder in the final round of the U.S. Open.

The ball veered left and stopped on the fringe of the green. Even though Chen had swung only four times, he lay in five, not four. He was so shaken by his stunning double flubble that he finished the hole with a horrendous quadruple-bogey eight.

Just like that, his four-stroke lead had vanished. He never regained it and lost the Open to Andy North by only one stroke.

In the locker room afterward, Chen spoke in broken English as he relived the awful moment that cost him the victory. "I open the face [of the club] and hit the ball soft to make the ball spin, but then I double-hit. I never hit a double before. It upset me a lot. It stay on my mind. I have stupid game today, but I can only blame me. Bad head."

Lloyd Mangrum

U.S. Open ■ June 11, 1950

Lloyd Mangrum got so bugged—literally—that he wound up losing the 1950 U.S. Open.

Battling for the lead in a tense play-off with Ben Hogan and George Fazio at the Merion Golf Club near Philadelphia, Mangrum trailed by only one stroke as the trio approached the green of the par four sixteenth hole. With his competitors on in two, Mangrum was lying in three and desperately needed to sink a fifteen-footer to save par.

After sighting the line of his putt, Mangrum noticed a gnat resting on his ball. The golfer waited for the insect to fly off, but it didn't. So he used the putter to mark the ball's position, picked the ball up, and blew on it until the offending gnat flew off. Then he put the ball back on the green and rolled it in for what he thought was a par. When

Hogan, the leader, also parred the hole, Mangrum assumed he was still only one stroke behind.

He was wrong. To his shock, Mangrum learned he was now three strokes behind. Isaac Grainger, chairman of the United States Golf Association's rules committee, had been sitting behind the green with the rest of the gallery. Grainger informed Mangrum that the golfer had broken a rule which states that you cannot lift a ball that is in play under penalty of two strokes. As good a pro as Mangrum was, he had never heard of the rule—until it was too late.

His ignorance of the rules took him completely out of the running for the championship. With only two holes remaining, he couldn't overcome his disastrous infraction and lost the play-off to Ben Hogan.

Sam Snead

U.S. Open ■ June 10, 1939

Sam Snead suffered the worst choke ever in a major tourney.

Early in his remarkable golfing career, Snead had all but wrapped up the victory in the 1939 U.S. Open on the Spring Mill course at the Philadelphia Country Club. He reached the seventy-first tee needing only a par and a bogey on the last two holes to beat the three leaders—including Byron Nelson, who was in the clubhouse at 284.

It looked like a cinch for Slammin' Sammy. But to his horror, Snead three-putted the seventy-first hole from only twenty feet out for a bogey. Even after that, all he had to do to win was shoot a par five on the last hole—an innocuous 558-yarder—just as he had easily done during the previous three rounds.

In those days, before leader boards, golfers didn't always know who was winning unless they asked one of the tournament officials. Incredibly, Snead never bothered to find out what score it would take to win. He just assumed that he had to birdie the hole for the lead. That meant he couldn't play it safe.

Battling his nerves, Sam powered his tee shot into the left rough. Then, convinced he had to reach the green in two, he boldly swatted a two-wood. But the ball drove into the sand up against the bank of a bunker 110 yards short of the green. He tried to blast the ball out with an eight-iron rather than a wedge, but the ball lodged in a crevice between two chunks of fresh sod which had been laid across the lip of the bunker. So Snead tried the same shot again with nearly the same dreaded result—the ball landed in another bunker forty yards from the green. Finally, he played a hit-and-hope shot, slashing his fifth stroke onto the green where the ball rolled dead fifty feet from the cup. Now Sam's only prayer was to tie with a miracle putt. And he made a great one, but the ball rimmed the cup and spun out.

Snead had lost the tournament that was his to win. In his black mood of anger and frustration, Sam didn't even try to line up the next putt, a three-footer, and he left it short. Then he tapped it in for the most infamous eight any pro ever had the misfortune to make.

That one hole haunted Snead for the rest of his otherwise spectacular golfing career.

Way Off Course

At the 1985 French Open, pro golfers Kent Kluba of the United States and Raphael Alarcon of Mexico experienced a duffer's nightmare —they got lost.

Because both golfers were unknown and had teed off early in the day, they played alone without anyone in the gallery watching them.

After completing the second hole, Kluba and Alarcon headed for what they thought was the third tee. Only after they had teed off and were lining up for their approach shot did they realize they were taking aim on the flag of the thirteenth green instead of the third hole. The accidental detour cost both golfers a two-stroke penalty— and plenty of clubhouse ribbing.

Bill Kratzert

Anheuser-Busch Golf Classic ■ July 11, 1986

Even the worst duffer who plunks tee shots in the water and hooks iron shots in the woods can usually finish a round of golf without running out of balls.

Not so for pro golfer Bill Kratzert, who was forced to withdraw from the Anheuser-Busch Golf Classic because he didn't have any balls left.

Kratzert's caddy, Jesse Douglas, had removed all the balls from Bill's bag after the first round because, he admitted, "the bag was too heavy and I didn't want to carry all that weight in this heat."

Before the start of the second round of the tournament in Williamsburg, Virginia, Kratzert didn't bother to check his bag. He simply handed his caddy a sleeve of three balls and began to play, wrongly assuming he had plenty more.

Bill played like he could have used a whole gross of balls. The thirty-four-year-old golfer drove his first ball into the water on the first hole, dumped another in the lake along the third green, and lost his third ball out of bounds on the seventh hole. But Kratzert's worst frustration came when he asked for another ball and his caddy replied, "I don't have any more."

PGA Tour rules prohibit a player from holding up play to get more balls or change types of ball during a round. Bill was too far away from the clubhouse to run over and buy a new supply. Neither playing partner Ken Green nor Kenny Knox were using the same kind of ball as Kratzert, so they couldn't loan him any.

Bill, who had shot a three-over-par 74 the day before to fall nine strokes behind the leader, had no choice but to withdraw. It was just as well. The way Kratzert was playing, he probably would have missed the cut anyway.

THE HOCKEY
HALL OF SHAME

Broad Street Bullies
(aka Philadelphia Flyers)

1972–75

With the carnage they spread throughout the NHL, the Broad Street Bullies might as well have played in spiked helmets and chains and carried switch blades and brass knuckles. Their style was nothing more than premeditated mayhem.

As the most high-sticking, spearing, slashing team ever to bloody the ice, the goons who were officially known as the Philadelphia Flyers led the league in knockdowns, knockouts, and penalty minutes. En route to their first Stanley Cup championship in 1974, the Flyers tallied a staggering total of 1,756 penalty minutes—*six hundred more than the next most-penalized team.* They fought at the drop of a puck and spent so much time in the penalty box that it looked like they had been forced to sign long-term leases. To opposing teams, a body check meant counting the casualties.

The Broad Street Bullies lived by the dubious creed of their scholarly looking coach Fred Shero. Known as "Ferocious Fred" in his playing days as a New York Ranger defenseman, Shero drummed into the Flyers' scarred heads such proverbs as "If you can't beat the other team in the alley, you can't beat them on ice" and "If you keep the opposition on their asses, they can't score points."

Shero often put his team through a drill that was brutal even by Philadelphia's no-holds-barred standards. One player was assigned to take a position in front of the goal and maintain it—while two others tried to mug him. The victim was supposed to prove his toughness by demonstrating his ability to keep his own bones from being broken.

The Flyers were skilled in the arts—of intimidation, brutality, and revenge. Bearded winger Bill "Cowboy" Fleet liked to give opposing rookies some helpful hints on the ice. "The first time you touch the puck," he'd tell them in a whisper, "I'll break your arm."

47

The Hammer nailing another opponent   AP/Wide World Photos

Touch one of the Flyers and there was no telling what would happen—on or off the ice. In a 1972 game in Vancouver, a young fan reached over the boards and foolishly yanked the hair of a Flyer. Within seconds, seven teammates charged into the stands wielding sticks and fists. They were later arrested and fined $500 apiece.

Revenge was the Bullies' middle name. In a 1973 game, California's Barry Cummins unwisely high-sticked Philadelphia captain Bobby Clarke across the head, opening a gash that required twenty stitches. The Flyers' goon squad immediately jumped into battle and mercilessly pummeled the attacker—until a bloodied Cummins had to be dragged off the ice by his teammates.

The way some of the Flyers played, you'd swear they had been recruited from an ad in *Soldier of Fortune* magazine. Bob "Hound" Kelly understood perfectly what his job as a hatchetman entailed. "They sure don't pay me to score goals," he once told the press. During the 1973–74 season, he scored only four goals in sixty-five games, but won fourteen of fifteen fights on the ice. "Kelly always gets in three or four punches before the other guy even realizes he's in a fight," marveled Clarke.

The chief hitman was Dave "The Hammer" Schultz, a beefy free-swinging wingman who set the record for most penalty minutes in one season with 472.

One of his finest moments came during a 1974 semifinal game against the Rangers. The Madison Square Garden crowd booed Schultz fervently when he charged onto the ice two minutes into the game and barreled full speed into Ranger defenseman Brad Park, knocking him down and nearly out. Straddling the dazed Park—who tried futilely to fight back—Schultz repeatedly slugged him in the face. The linesman finally pulled Schultz off Park, but while Park was still supine—held down, in fact, by one of the officials who was trying to stop the fight—Schultz belted him with four successive shots to the stomach. The Hammer was nailed with a two-minute roughing penalty, a two-minute charging penalty, and a five-minute fighting penalty. When Park received only a five-minute fighting penalty, Schultz gave a choke signal to the referee, who in turn slapped Schultz with a ten-minute misconduct rap. In one vicious play, Schultz racked up four penalties totaling nineteen minutes. "I get so worked up I don't know what's going on," confessed Schultz.

Shero made no bones about Schultz's value to the team. "Speed, skill, and strength make a hockey player," said the coach. "Schultz realizes he does not have speed or skill, so what is he here for? To beat up the other guy."

It was a rare compliment from the taciturn coach. To keep his players tough, Shero almost never said a good word about them. "That's just the way I am," he said. "I told my wife 'I love you' once—and that was the day we were married."

Jim Stewart

Goalie ■ Boston Bruins ■ January 10, 1980

It was a good thing Boston Bruins rookie Jim Stewart wore a face mask. It hid his embarrassment after he made the most inauspicious NHL debut ever for a goalie.

Boston found itself short of puck stoppers when both regulars Gerry Cheevers and Gilles Gilbert were sidelined. So just twelve hours after the team called up Stewart from Utica of the Eastern League, he was tending the nets in Boston in a game against the St. Louis Blues. Stewart had dreamed about this moment ever since he graduated from Holy Cross. He had seen himself snaring slap shots with his glove, deflecting rebounds with his stick, and making the big save. Unfortunately, he was not clairvoyant.

The way Stewart played, the Bruins would have been better off pulling the goalie at the opening face-off. He let three of the first four shots get by him. The Zamboni had barely motored out of the rink before Stewart blew his first chance at a save. Just 1:08 into the game, the Blues' Brian Sutter fired a fifty-foot slap shot by Stewart's left. Less than two minutes later, Bernie Federko of St. Louis faked a pass, deeked the goalie out of position, and flipped the puck into the net. It took only fifty-one seconds for the Blues to score again as Mike Crombeen put a backhander through the rookie's legs from up close. In Stewart's first three minutes, forty-six seconds of NHL goaltending, he had given up *three* goals.

He settled down and shut out St. Louis for nearly twelve minutes before Sutter scored his second goal of the period, sailing the puck through Stewart's legs. About a minute later, at 16:42, Crombeen nailed his second goal when he whacked in his own rebound.

Stewart slip sliding away   *Boston Globe* Photo

At the end of the first period, Stewart had stopped only four of nine shots on goal as the Bruins trailed 5–2. Boston coach Fred Creighton had seen more than enough and replaced Stewart with another rookie, Marco Baron, who surrendered two goals in the last two periods in a 7–4 Bruins loss.

In the dressing room after the game, Stewart was surrounded by media people and, with three microphones shoved under his chin, he smiled and asked with wide-eyed innocence, "What's it like when we win?"

He claimed he wasn't scared in his debut. "I felt great in the pregame warmups and I didn't think I was nervous, but I must have been. Nothing went right from the first shot on. I couldn't stop a basketball. Three of their goals went through my legs and twice I moved too quickly. It was some kind of a shock to be here."

It certainly was no shock for fans and players when Stewart was quickly shipped back to Utica. He never played in the NHL again.

Montreal Wanderers

February 1906

It took all season for the Montreal Wanderers to win the Stanley Cup, yet it took only a few hours for them to lose professional hockey's most treasured prize.

Immediately after winning the championship in 1906, the Wanderers (no relation to the Canadiens) boozed it up at a party before deciding to have a photo taken of themselves with the coveted silver trophy.

With the players well into the grape, they staggered over to Jimmy Rice's Famous Studio where they held up the Cup and smiled for the camera. Then they headed for a nearby bar to celebrate for a few more hours. But in all their revelry, they forgot to take the very thing they had worked so hard to win. They left the Cup behind on a chair in the corner of the now-empty studio.

Apparently, everyone on the team assumed that someone else had the trophy. Not until the beginning of the next hockey season did management realize the Cup was missing. An all-points bulletin was issued throughout Montreal as a mad search for the trophy began.

One of the players recalled last seeing the Cup at the photo studio. But owner Jimmy Rice said he hadn't seen it since the night he took the team's picture. On a hunch, Rice asked his cleaning lady if she had any idea where the Cup might be. After hearing his detailed description of it, she said, "Oh, is *that* what it is."

She then explained what happened to the Cup. A few hours after the team had left the studio, she was cleaning up the place when she came across this lovely silver cup. Figuring it wasn't doing any good sitting in the corner, she took it home and put it to some good, practical use. She filled it with potting soil, planted some geraniums in it, and placed it on her windowsill. And there it stayed throughout the summer. Somewhat sadly, the woman returned the trophy to the team—minus the geraniums.

The Stanley Cup may be hockey's Holy Grail, but thanks to the carelessness of the Montreal Wanderers, it turned into nothing more than a cleaning lady's flowerpot.

The Stanley Cup Runneth into Trouble

Other Ways Hockey's Famed Trophy Has Been Abused

• 1905—Drop-kicked into river. Hours after winning Cup, Ottawa Silver Seven got drunk and during revelry booted trophy into frozen Rideau Canal. Next morning, hungover captain Harry Smith found it still sitting atop ice.

• 1924—Abandoned on street. After victory party, Montreal Canadiens were driving home with Cup when their car stalled on hill. Players got out to push after setting trophy by curb. When they reached top of hill, players jumped back into car and drove off. Hour later, they raced back to hill and recovered lost silver.

• 1962—Stolen by Canadiens fan. Chicago Black Hawks, 1961 winners, displayed Cup in unlocked case in Chicago Stadium lobby during 1962 play-offs against Montreal. Furious that trophy resided in Windy City, Canadiens fan Ken Kilander opened case, took Cup, and nonchalantly walked toward street when apprehended by security guard. Said Kilander before police whisked him to jail, "I want to take it back to Montreal—where it belongs!"

Philadelphia Flyers vs. Buffalo Sabres

"The Fog Game"

May 20, 1975

During the third game of the 1975 Stanley Cup finals, the players skated like they were in a fog.

That's because they *were* in a fog—one so thick that it would have kept the U.S. Navy in port.

The visiting Philadelphia Flyers and the Buffalo Sabres played under the worst conditions ever in NHL play-off history. For starters, the game was held so late in the season that the weather had turned hot. This was a serious problem because Buffalo's Memorial Stadium was not air conditioned. As a result, the teams battled in stifling heat and oppressive humidity that melted patches of ice into puddles and spread a thick, waist-high fog throughout the league's smallest rink.

The game was delayed eleven times because of the pea soup. During each unscheduled intermission, the players were sent out en masse to circle the arena and stir up the dead air. The only players who weren't annoyed by the delays were the benchwarmers, who received more ice time than ever before.

It was one of those you-have-to-see-it-to-believe-it games. Unfortunately, most of the fans at the game *couldn't* see it; they could only hear the slapping of the puck against the sticks and boards.

However bad it was for the fans, conditions were worse for the players. The rink was a foggy hotbox that slowed the once-swift skaters; their tired legs proved unable to rush the puck up the ice by the end of the game. "It was so bloody hot out there it was unbearable," complained Flyer defenseman Ed Van Impe.

"Some of the guys took their (long john) underwear off after the third period because it was so wet and heavy from sweat," said Flyer assistant coach Barry Ashbee.

Fittingly, in the eerie setting of the heat and fog, a small bat swept down from the upper reaches of the arena and buzzed the rink. But Buffalo's Jim Lorentz high-sticked it to death and Philly's Rick MacLeish dropped it in the penalty box, adding a bizarre touch to the game.

As luck would have it, the Sabres and Flyers wearily skated into overtime for an extra eighteen minutes before Buffalo's Gilbert Perreault and Rene Robert came out of the fog like deadly phantoms into the Philadelphia zone. Perreault fired a shot into the corner while the Flyers were in the midst of a line change. The puck ricocheted to Robert, who blasted a twenty-four-footer. Flyers goalie Bernie Parent, who could barely make out the shadowy figures in the middle of the ice, never moved. "I didn't have the foggiest notion where the puck was until it was too late," he said. By the time Parent reacted, the puck from Robert's slap shot crashed into the net—and the Sabres had defeated the Flyers, 5–4.

"Four or five times the Sabres came down with the puck and I couldn't see who had it," said Parent. "I'm surprised the game didn't end sooner. I'll put some windshield wipers on my mask for the next time."

When the fog returned during the next game (which Buffalo won 4–2 to tie the championship series), the Sabre management unveiled a revolutionary, if primitive new system for fog control. Five teams of arena attendants, each armed with a bed sheet, skated around the ice and waved off the fog.

When the Flyers returned home to the air-conditioned Spectrum, they played in unlimited visibility and drubbed the Sabres to win the Stanley Cup.

Although the Buffalo pea soup created a scene more in keeping with an Edgar Allan Poe tale than an NHL play-off clash, Philly coach Fred Shero said conditions weren't quite as terrible as those in a game in Houston in 1948. "It was so bad," he recalled, "that we were on our hands and knees looking for the puck. We couldn't find it, so they called the game."

Rinky Dink Justice

The NHL, in its ever-vigilant quest to tame the shocking amount of violence on the ice, slipped badly during a blood bath between the California Seals and Toronto Maple Leafs.

Battling in Oakland on February 19, 1975, the teams went after each other as if they were reenacting the Crimean War. One fallen player was carted off on a stretcher during the fight-marred game. At one point, most everyone in the stadium was shocked when two mayhem-minded players bashed each other with their sticks, and yet no penalty was called.

However, when an outraged fan hurled an empty ice cream container at one of the referees, the fan was quickly hauled out of the stands—and booked for assault and battery!

Nick Polano   Glen Sonmor

Coach ■ Detroit Red Wings   Coach ■ Minnesota North Stars
February 14, 1985

Fisticuffs in hockey are as common as slap shots. But the slugfest between the Detroit Red Wings and Minnesota North Stars was a breakaway from the norm because both coaches wrestled with each other—and were joined in the fray by a former pro football coach.

The brawl broke out at the aptly named Joe Louis Arena in Detroit at the end of the first period. As the teams skated off the ice, Danny Gare of the Wings and Dino Ciccarelli of the North Stars used the Detroit bench for a boxing ring. It quickly became crowded with players from both sides, including Detroit goalie Greg Stefan, who was sitting behind the bench in street clothes that night.

That infuriated Minnesota coach Glen Sonmor. "I saw a guy in street clothes grabbing and punching away at a couple of our guys on the Detroit bench," Sonmor later told the press. "If you think I'm going to stand there and watch crap like that, you don't know me."

As he tried to run across the ice, Sonmor fell, and his backup goalie Don Beaupre stepped on the coach's right hand, producing a cut that needed sixteen stitches. Despite the injury, Sonmor charged after Stefan. At the bench, Detroit coach Nick Polano pushed Sonmor back and the two squared off for a fight of their own. "Glen is fifty-four years old, wears glasses, and was bleeding from the hand," Polano recounted. "I was trying to calm him down. I told him, 'This job is hard enough. You don't need this.'" But when the combative Sonmor was joined by North Star Harold Snepsts, the short-handed Polano dropped the olive branch and put up his dukes.

Suddenly, a fan swept into action like Clark Kent, without stopping at the phone booth to change. The fan was Monte Clark, the 6-foot, 6-inch, 270-pound former coach of the Detroit Lions, who raced from his seat to the Wings' bench. With one arm, Clark jerked Polano out of the pile of players, and with the other, he grabbed Tiger Williams of the Wings and hustled them off to the dressing room.

"I was just pitching in and helping some Detroit people," said Clark, an NFL offensive lineman for eleven years. "Nick was trying to be a peacemaker until someone wanted a piece of him. I just thought I'd get him out of there so he wouldn't get thrown out. That other coach [Sonmor] looked like he was going berserk. He looked like a madman."

When the round ended, referee Ron Wicks ejected three North Stars, three Red Wings, Stefan, and Sonmor. In the game, which ended in a 5–5 tie, the ref handed out 149 penalty minutes, including ninety-four for the big brawl.

Afterward, Polano said he appreciated Clark's help. "I didn't know who grabbed me and pulled me backward, but I knew he was strong," said the coach. "I was glad to find out he was on my side." Asked if Clark gave him any sage words, Polano said, "He told me, 'You hockey people are crazy.'"

Steve Smith

Defenseman ■ Edmonton Oilers ■ April 30, 1986

If ever there was a time Steve Smith wished the ice could crack beneath his skates and swallow him up, it was in the last period of a deciding game in the 1986 Stanley Cup play-offs.

Smith committed a blunder so costly and astounding that he became an instant soulmate of such legendary bunglers as Fred "Bonehead" Merkle and Roy "Wrong Way" Riegels.

The Edmonton Oilers, gunning for their third straight Stanley Cup, had rallied from a 2–0 deficit to tie the Calgary Flames 2–2 in the third period of the seventh and deciding game of the Smythe Division finals in Edmonton.

There were less than six minutes left in regulation play when Smith made the most unforgettably inept pass in Stanley Cup history. The Oilers' rookie defenseman, playing a regular shift because of an injury to veteran Lee Fogolin, attempted a routine clearing pass from behind the corner of his own net. But the puck hit the back of the ankle of his teammate, goaltender Grant Fuhr, and skipped right into the Edmonton net for a stunning goal. When Smith realized what he had done, he dropped to his knees and hung his head in shame. Calgary's left wing, Perry Berezan, the closest opponent to the net, was credited with the goal with 5:14 remaining in the game. Fired up by the unexpected goal, the Flames held on for an upset 3–2 victory.

Afterward, in the stunned Oilers' locker room, a teary-eyed Smith said, "I just tried to make a quick play with a guy bearing down on me. I got good wood on it. It's just that it didn't go in the direction I wanted. It's the worst feeling I've ever had in my life. Sooner or later I've got to face it. But at least it's not the end of the world."

No, but it was the end of Edmonton's season, as the two-time NHL champions were ousted from the Stanley Cup play-offs.

Of all the days to screw up, wouldn't you know it happened on Smith's twenty-third birthday. Apparently he forgot that birthday boys are supposed to receive gifts—not give them.

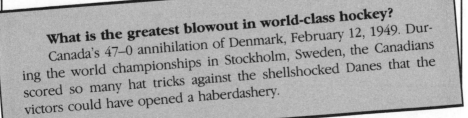

What is the greatest blowout in world-class hockey?
Canada's 47–0 annihilation of Denmark, February 12, 1949. During the world championships in Stockholm, Sweden, the Canadians scored so many hat tricks against the shellshocked Danes that the victors could have opened a haberdashery.

Truth in Advertising

How do you lay out the welcome mat for fans of the NHL's doormat? By creating an ad campaign that promotes shame.

In 1974, the dismal Washington Capitals won only eight games, tied five, and lost an incredible sixty-seven. For the following year, club officials had to create an ad that would attract fans. So the Caps came up with an approach that was as strange as it was forthright:

"For as little as $4 a ticket," the ad said, "the least you'll feel is reasonably disappointed . . . Last year, everybody frequently expected the Capitals to lose. And we did lose. Frequently . . . We're going to win a lot more games this year than we won last year. It would be hard not to . . ."

Gilles Gratton

Goalie ■ St. Louis Blues–New York Rangers ■ 1975–77

When it came to injuries, Gilles Gratton skated on pretty thin ice. And nobody ever believed him—perhaps with good reason.

In six starts with the St. Louis Blues, Gratton took himself out of two games that he was losing after being hit on the arm by a puck. Never mind that getting struck on the arm is an everyday occupational irritant that well-padded goalies almost always shake off, if they feel it at all.

His teammates were convinced that the more he cried foul, the more he cried wolf. This was especially true in his seventh—and last—start for the Blues. With the game scoreless in the first period, New York Islander Bob Nystrom lifted a soft backhanded shot. The puck floated toward the St. Louis goal and struck Gratton on the right arm with the impact of a jelly donut. But Gratton acted as if he had been shot with a .357 Magnum. He fell to the ice, writhed and rolled in pain and, at his insistence, was helped to the bench by the trainer.

His teammates were not amused. They knew that 999 of 1,000 goalies would have rubbed their arms and returned to the crease. Unfortunately, they were saddled with a one-in-a-thousand goaltender. But not for long. Coach Garry Young told him, "I never want to see you again." So Gratton went home and didn't return to the NHL until four months later when the New York Rangers obtained him.

Gratton brought new life—or more accurately, previous lives—into his brief career with the Rangers. Gratton was a strong believer in reincarnation and told his new teammates that he had lived hundreds of lives—some of which he said still affected his physical condition.

Before one Ranger game, Gratton went up to coach John Ferguson and announced that he couldn't play because of a leg injury. When the coach asked him how he hurt his leg, Gratton replied, "I was a soldier in the Franco-Prussian War of 1870 and was wounded in the leg. It still bothers me from time to time."

Octopus-Throwers

Detroit Red Wing Fans

In the most disgusting tradition in hockey, Detroit Red Wing fans flung octopuses onto the ice during home games of the Stanley Cup play-offs.

This bizarre custom began during the 1952 play-offs, when rabid Red Wing fans Pete Cusimano and his brother Jerry wanted to come up with a good luck charm for the team.

"My dad was in the fish and poultry business," Pete recalled, "and my brother and I helped him. Often after work, we'd go to the Red Wing games. Anyway, after the Red Wings won seven play-off games in a row, in 1952, my brother suggested, 'Why don't we throw an octopus on the ice for good luck? It's got eight legs and that might be a good omen.'"

On April 15, 1952, Jerry tossed his first octopus onto the ice of the Detroit Olympia. The dead octopus weighed about three pounds, was partially boiled to turn it a deep red, and was quite smelly. "You ever smelled a half-boiled octopus?" Pete asked. "It ain't exactly Chanel No. 5, you know." It ain't exactly what referee Frank Udvari had expected to see in a hockey game. "You should have seen how high Udvari jumped when he saw our first octopus!" said Pete.

Ever since that first toss—the Wings beat Montreal to win the Stanley Cup—Pete or his brother Jerry threw an octopus at least once in every Detroit play-off series for the next fifteen years.

To a group of intrigued reporters, Pete demonstrated his octopus-throwing technique. "You grip the thing in the palm of your hand," he explained. "You pick out your target. Then you rear back and heave it like you would a hand grenade. You've got to keep your elbow stiff to get the the best distance."

He said he seldom tried to throw an octopus at a specific target. "I look on the whole ice surface as my strike zone. But one time I got hot at Ted Kennedy of the Toronto Maple Leafs. He'd been having a big series against the Wings. So during a beef, when they were all standing around arguing, I decided to let him have it. Only I hit another Toronto player. Vic Lynn was standing right beside Kennedy and Vic got the octopus. Splat in the kisser!"

When the Red Wings began missing the play-offs on a regular basis throughout much of the 1970s, Detroit's octopus population was spared. But in 1978, that reprieve ended. While the Red Wings were winning their second straight game against the favored Atlanta Flames in the opening round of the play-offs, deliriously happy Detroit fans hurled no fewer than a dozen *live* octopuses onto the ice.

As a result, Olympia maintenance crews kept scurrying around the rink with pails and shovels while the more mannerly fans in the crowd wondered whether there might not be a more tasteful way of saluting Detroit's hockey revival.

Other spectators agreed—and began bombarding the ice with such things as two dead chickens, dead fish, and scores of apples. There were moments when the inside of the Olympia looked as littered as the floor of a meat and produce market after a sale.

For the quarterfinals against the Montreal Canadiens, the rowdier fans decided to follow tradition in a big way. From all corners of the stadium, octopuses went flying through the air. An official count claimed forty-three of the cephalopods went crashing onto the ice with sickening thwacks in one game alone. As a result, the maintenance crew was on the ice almost as much as the players.

Canadiens' coach Scotty Bowman wore a helmet given by one of his players near the end of a 4–2 victory over Detroit to avoid getting hit with a dead octopus.

Admitted Red Wings coach Bobby Kromm after the game, "One octopus or two is OK, but tonight was a little much."

What NHL hockey player was sent to the penalty box for kissing a puck?

Randy Pierce, right wing of the Colorado Rockies. In the final minute of a 7–4 win over the New York Islanders on November 28, 1979, Pierce scored an insurance goal and was so pleased with himself that he retrieved the puck, kissed it, and tossed it over the glass. He was assessed a two-minute penalty for delay of game.

New York Rangers

January 23, 1944

In the most lopsided score in NHL history, the New York Rangers were clobbered 15–0 by the Detroit Red Wings.

The goal light flashed on so many times that hapless New York goalie Ken "Tubby" McAuley got a suntan. His goaltending shortcomings weren't to blame so much as was the ineptness of the sievelike Ranger defense, which allowed Detroit an incredible fifty-eight shots on goal. To his credit, McAuley stopped forty-three of them. To his discredit, he let 15 get by him, the most ever in one game.

In front of 12,293 delighted fans at Detroit's Olympia, every player on the Red Wings—except defenseman Cully Simon and goalie Connie Dion either scored or got an assist. The Rangers turned losing into an art form. It took Detroit only three minutes to score its first goal. Then, while they were shorthanded, the Red Wings passed the puck to each other for ninety seconds without a single Ranger touching it. When New York's Bryan Hextall finally got his stick on it, Detroit's Flash Hollett spun him around with a check and dished off a quick pass to Bill Quackenbush, who slapped in a ten-footer for a 2–0 lead. The rout was on.

In the second period, down 3–0, the Rangers gave an impersonation of the London blitz by getting bombed with four goals in just six minutes. By the final stanza, it was clear that McAuley would have been better off in front of a firing squad. At least there, he'd have been shot at only once. Firing pucks with machine gun ferocity, the Red Wings racked up a never-before-seen eight goals in the third period.

The bloodthirsty Detroit fans screamed themselves hoarse for more. They almost got their wish for a sixteenth goal. As the last few seconds ticked off, three Wings broke away without a Ranger between them and McAuley. They passed the puck back and forth to bewilder the goalie—and to give each other an assist point. But they dallied too long. Just a second before Carl Liscombe fired the puck into the net at point-blank range, the green light flashed, ending the massacre.

"I was so mad after the game, I didn't want to talk to anybody," recalled McAuley. "I came into the dressing room and I was burning. (New York defenseman) Bucko McDonald came over to me and said, 'Hey, don't let it worry you. There've been a lot of goalies in this league and none of them ever set a record.'"

The slaughter turned things around for the Rangers. Instead of a pattern of losing two and winning one, they went on a remarkable streak—they failed to win their next twenty-five games. Needless to say, New York finished last in a dismal season that saw McAuley set a futility mark that still stands—he gave up an average of six goals a game.

However, some good did come out of the Detroit debacle, according to McAuley. "Where would all those Red Wing players have been without me? I gave 'em the confidence they needed to become big stars," he said after the shameful rout.

Boston Bruins vs. Minnesota North Stars

February 26, 1981

With all their headhunters and their spearing and slashing, the NHL's most vicious hockey game should have been played in the world's deepest, darkest jungle.

Instead, the anarchy on ice unfolded in Boston where the Bruins and Minnesota North Stars took the term "attacking zone" much too literally. In the most penalty-marred game in history, the teams were whistled for a record eighty-four penalties totaling a whopping 406 penalty minutes. That's an average of one penalty every forty-three seconds and 6.8 penalty minutes for every minute played.

In all, twelve players—seven North Stars and five Bruins—were thrown out of the game for fighting. Time and again, the ice was littered with gloves as both benches cleared out for bare-knuckle brawling. The three harried referees didn't have the manpower or muscle to break up the donnybrooks. Before the night was over and Boston had won 5–1, six penalty records had been set.

Fans hadn't even settled in their seats when the first fight broke out only seven seconds into the game. Boston's Steve Kasper and Minnesota's Bobby Smith mixed it up and were slapped with seven minutes in penalties. However, Keith Crowder of the Bruins and Steve Payne of the North Stars had also joined the fray. Payne was nailed with a twenty-minute misconduct penalty for throwing punches from behind referee Dave Newell, who was trying to separate the combatants.

More fisticuffs broke out less than three minutes later, followed

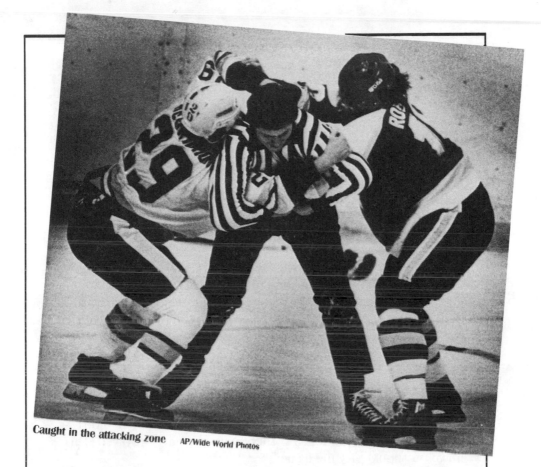

Caught in the attacking zone   AP/Wide World Photos

by another melee at 3:35 which left Boston with only four men on the ice and six in the penalty box. The sin bin was so crowded that the attendant had to move out.

The worst and biggest brawl erupted at 8:58 in the first period when players from both sides dropped their gloves and duked it out at center ice. The officials then began ejecting one player after another. As the banished North Stars headed for their locker room, they went by the Boston bench where they traded slurs with the Bruins. Once again, they slugged it out—only this time some of the Boston fans jumped in and threw a few punches before a handful of security guards broke it up.

At one point a few minutes later, the Bruins and North Stars had only six players each on the bench, with others either in the penalty box or banished to the dressing room. A club normally has nineteen players in uniform.

The first stanza fighting set records for most penalties in one period—sixty-seven—and most penalties by one team in one period, thirty-four by Minnesota. The most-penalized player was the Bruins' Brad McCrimmon, who received a double major penalty and a total of thirty minutes.

The North Stars said after the game that they had been told by their coach, Glen Sonmor, to be more physical against the Bruins. Apparently, the team took his words to heart. "Sure, I told my guys I was tired of us being pushed around," Sonmor said of his team, which had not won in the Boston Garden in thirty-five games. "I told them I wanted them to do something—not the second time they're victims of a cheap shot, not the third, but the first."

Boston's Brad Park claimed Minnesota started the fighting and forced the Bruins to defend themselves. "What do you do if somebody challenges you in front of 14,000 people?" he asked. "Do you back away? Their coach told them to play rough. That sounds premeditated to me. Ask yourself, 'Who's at fault? The players or the coach?'"

Added Bruins coach Gerry Cheevers, "When somebody like [mild-mannered] Bobby Smith starts fighting at seven seconds, you know something is going on. But fighting is part of hockey. I didn't see anything violent about tonight. There were no sticks involved. This is how you should play the game."

The league didn't see it that way. Of the twelve players ejected, several received fines and suspensions for fighting among themselves and for jostling the refs who were trying to break up the brawls.

Even after the game was over, the two coaches continued the hostilities with a shouting match and scuffle under the stands. Before he was pulled away by security guards, Sonmor challenged Cheevers to a fight at their next game against each other. Snarled Sonmor in a parting shot, "You'd better bring a basket—for your head!"

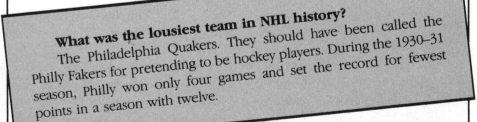

What was the lousiest team in NHL history?
The Philadelphia Quakers. They should have been called the Philly Fakers for pretending to be hockey players. During the 1930–31 season, Philly won only four games and set the record for fewest points in a season with twelve.

THE TENNIS HALL OF SHAME

Ilie Nastase

U.S. Open ■ August 30, 1979

Forest Hills tennis umpire Adrian Clark once said, "When Ilie Nastase is winning, he's objectionable. When he's losing, he's highly objectionable."

Nastase—the clown prince of tennis—proved Clark right during the 1979 U.S. Open at the National Tennis Center. Egging on a beered-up crowd with his patented boorish behavior, Nastase triggered the ugliest incident in the history of American tennis.

When the thirty-three-year-old, hot-tempered Romanian played then twenty-year-old apprentice brat John McEnroe in the second round of the Open, a fan had scribbled a sign that read, "This tennis match has been rated R. No one under 17 admitted without a parent or guardian."

The last time the two *enfants terribles* met, Nasty rubbed cigarette ashes on his nose to mock a scab that McEnroe had on his. They spent the entire match needling each other and argued in the locker room afterward.

They continued their bickering in their U.S. Open match. From the outset, Nastase was the crowd's favorite. McEnroe's errors and double faults were cheered, and he responded with taunts, all of which was fine with Nastase. What didn't please him was McEnroe's slow play. 'A player is allowed thirty seconds between points, and McEnroe seemed to be taking the full thirty.

Ilie responded by chatting informally with spectators, pretending to nap behind the baseline, and quick-serving McEnroe. When umpire Frank Hammond warned Nastase for stalling in the second set, the crowd sided with Nastase as he lay on the ground, racquet perched behind his head.

He continued to play up to the 10,549 spectators until, after lingering in the back court for nearly a minute, he was slapped with a point penalty which gave McEnroe the fifth game of the third set and a

3–2 lead. Ilie exploded in anger, ranting and raving at Hammond. "I've protected you as much as I can!" the umpire shouted down from his chair loud enough for all to hear. "You play tennis like everyone else!"

Reluctantly, the Romanian returned to the court, but he continued to play his childish stalling games. Finally, in the fourth set, after further warnings, Hammond penalized Nastase a full game for stalling with McEnroe serving at 2–1, 15–0. When the crowd realized that the game penalty gave McEnroe a 3–1 lead, they showered the umpire with ear-numbing boos and jeers. Nastase fueled their ire by refusing to serve. For the next seventeen minutes, the court had all the ambience of a back-alley brawl. Fights broke out among fans, beer cans and other debris were hurled onto the court, screaming spectators leaped out of the stands, and hecklers shouted obscenities at the players and Hammond. Police surrounded the court, and Hammond and tournament referee Mike Blanchard pleaded with Nastase to

Nastase working on his ground stroke   Marilynn K. Yee/NYT Pictures

resume play. When he refused, Blanchard told him he had thirty seconds to serve. After fifty-eight seconds, Hammond—following the rules of tennis—announced "Game, set, match, McEnroe." At that moment, tournament director Bill Talbert approached the chair, rescinded the default, and ordered Blanchard to take Hammond's place to restore order and avoid a riot. "In forty-eight years of tennis, I've never seen anything like it," lamented Talbert, a former high-ranked player and Davis Cup captain. Although McEnroe could have walked off the court and taken the victory on the disqualification, he agreed to play out the match once Nastase was coaxed back onto the court. McEnroe then polished off Ilie fair-and-square, 6–4, 4–6, 6–3, 6–2.

This wasn't the first time Nastase deliberately showed up Hammond. Once while Hammond umpired a match between Ilie and Bob Hewitt in the grandstand court, Hewitt got angry at himself for losing a game point. He socked the ball up into the air so hard that it landed about seven courts away where a doubles match was taking place. Hammond ordered Hewitt to keep his cool.

Recalled Hammond, "At this point Nastase said, 'Well, now *I've* got one coming.' Sure enough, a couple of games later, he smacked a ball in a fit of rage—very likely faked—and it soared way up and hit a guy who was leaning over and looking down from the parapet of the stadium next door. It actually hit this guy right in the middle of the forehead. Really popped him."

Linda Siegel

Wimbledon ■ May 29, 1979

For everyone who plays at Wimbledon, it's the championship or bust. For Linda Siegel, it was bust—in every sense of the word.

The eighteen-year-old Californian played in a tennis outfit so daringly low-cut that during a match her breasts fell out, giving the staid English crowd a stunning display of her form.

Linda was battling Billie Jean King in a second-round match when she first exposed herself to serious trouble. During a change of sides, Linda bent over near the umpire's stand and realized that she was coming out of the top of her tennis dress. "I kept hanging a towel around my neck to make sure nothing happened," she recalled. "But when I got back on the court, everything just fell out."

The crowd tittered and then broke into guffaws when a spectator shouted, "Now that's what I call a deuce!" Wearing little more than an embarrassed smile, the bare-chested tennis player stuffed herself back into her outfit. Although Linda held onto her cool, she lost the match 6–1, 6–3. Afterward, when asked by reporters what she thought of the revealing dress, Billie Jean said, "If endowed, wear it."

The next day, the front pages of several British tabloids prominently displayed photos of Linda spilling out of her outfit. The conservative *Daily Telegraph* reported, "The lawn tennis was not spectacular, but Miss Siegel, needing to make some essential adjustments, did not learn of the strategic value of a pin."

The flashy *Daily Mail* said that Linda's eye-popping dress "kept all heads turned one way" in wait for the fallout. Finally, "Linda's dress—bra-less, back-less, and, as she admitted later, a bit reckless— could take the strain no longer. Linda clearly was out."

Hinting that she had launched a new tennis fad, *The Evening Standard* ran a photo of four women in topless outfits marching onto center court with their racquets under their arms. The caption read, "I heard [tennis dress designer] Teddy Tinling was up all night making them."

So what was the result of all this publicity? Linda was asked to pose nude for another tabloid.

This being her very first Wimbledon, Linda had wanted to make a lasting impression. That she did. Veteran observers said that of all the debuts they had ever seen, hers was the breast.

Double Trouble

Miss M.H. de Amorin of Brazil played only two rounds at Wimbledon in 1957—but she left a lasting impression in the record book. Her service was so horrendous that had she been a waitress she wouldn't have received a penny in tips. Amorin began her match against Mrs. L.B.E. Thung of Holland by serving an incredible seventeen successive double faults! Playing as though the net belonged in a volleyball game, Amorin lost the match 6–3, 4–6, 6–1.

Hank Pfister

National 21-and-Unders Tournament ■ June 27, 1976

Hank Pfister had his ground stroke in tune, but what he wound up needing most during one major amateur tournament was a strong swim stroke.

Before Pfister became a world-ranked tennis pro, he was a Junior Davis Cup player who competed in the 1976 National 21-and-Unders tourney held in New York City. Hank made it into the finals, where he won the first two sets but then dropped the next two. When he lost his serve in the first game of the fifth set, Hank was so ticked off at himself that he threw his tennis racquet up in the air.

"I had no intention of throwing it over the fence," Pfister recalled, "but it hit the top of the fence and bounced over. The courts were situated right on the banks of the East River and wouldn't you know the racquet struck some rocks below and then went right into the river.

"So even though there were about 1,500 people in the stands, I halted play and went after my racquet. I went down to the edge of the water and tried to reach out for the racquet, but I missed it. The current was carrying it farther down the river and I figured I had one more chance. I took one step into the water and went straight down. The river bank didn't angle out into the water so I wound up totally under water. When I got back to the surface, I grabbed my racquet and swam back to shore.

"The East River is not exactly the cleanest river in the world and when I returned to the court dripping wet, I had green gunk hanging all over me. The crowed went nuts and cheered and laughed. The umpire didn't know whether to default me or not. Finally he said, 'Let's play.' I had been out on the court for four hours, had blown a two-set-to-love lead, and taken a swim in the East River, so I wasn't in the best frame of mind. I got another racquet and finished the set—and lost the match.

"It was definitely shameful. But now as I look back on the whole thing, it sure was funny."

Ivan Lendl   Jimmy Connors

Volvo Masters   **Lipton International**
January 16, 1981   **February 21, 1986**

Ivan Lendl and Jimmy Connors have trumpeted the virtues of hard work and maximum effort on every point. But they hit sour notes in two of their matches against each other—Lendl for tanking and Connors for quitting.

During the 1981 Volvo Masters at Madison Square Garden, Lendl discovered that it paid to lose. Because of a round-robin format, the winner of his quarterfinal match with Connors would play Bjorn Borg while the loser would face Gene Mayer. By losing, Lendl figured he would likely beat the lower-ranked Mayer and gain entry into the finals. That would assure Lendl of pocketing at least an extra $35,000 for second place. On the other side of the net, defeating Connors would give Lendl the "privilege" of playing Borg, who at the time was virtually unbeatable.

Not wanting to lose out on the thirty-five grand, the Czech appeared to play for the good of his wallet rather than for the good of tennis. Against Connors, Ivan sprayed easy shots all over the place, exposing his "losing edge" to a jeering, heckling crowd of 15,785 who knew a tank job when they saw one. Lendl was routed 7–6, 6–1, winning only six points in the first five games of the second set.

Connors, fuming at Ivan's deliberately poor showing throughout the match, let the fans know he was disgusted. After the match, he shook hands with Lendl at the net without looking at him and then made a derogatory gesture.

As everyone figured, Lendl trounced Mayer while Borg dispatched Connors in the semis. Borg then beat Lendl in the final. Because of Lendl's scandalous play, tournament officials changed the rules the following year so that losing was no longer profitable.

After the tourney, an angry Connors told the press that Lendl's performance was "chicken" and that he himself played to win all the time. But Jimmy can't make that claim anymore.

At the 1986 Lipton International Players Championships in Boca Raton, Florida, Connors simply quit—there's no other word for it. In the fifth set of a tense semifinal match, Lendl was leading 3–2, 30–0 when a close call went Ivan's way. Connors lost all control. He stormed umpire Jeremy Shale's chair, ranting and screaming. He demanded to see the tournament referee. Getting no satisfaction from Shales, Connors sat petulantly as the umpire penalized him a point, which gave Lendl the game and a 4–2 lead. Connors still refused to play and received a game penalty, making the score 5–2. When he refused to budge, officials announced a default. With that, Connors packed his bags and stalked off the court. For his childish action, he was fined $5,000.

"I don't think a player should default on a bad call," said Lendl afterward. "We've had thousands of them before."

Perhaps it was just as well that Connors quit. Lendl had won eight consecutive matches against him.

Jimmy proving some boys never grow up   UPI/Bettmann Newsphotos

Italian Fans

Italian Open ■ May 1978

The crowd at the Italian Open is sometimes like bubbling spaghetti sauce—too hot to handle and loaded with meatballs.

Normally sane and civilized Italian fans turn into wild lunatics when one of their countrymen makes it into the late rounds. They harass the Italian's opponent by hurling disruptive invectives, catcalls, coins, and cans. At least back in the days of the Coliseum the Christians only had to contend with the lions, not the spectators.

The Italian Open is held in Rome at the Foro Italico, a statue-bedecked tennis facility built by Il Duce himself, Benito Mussolini, in the mid-1930s. It is here that refugees from soccer brawls, teenage tennis groupies, and Italians afflicted with nationalistic fever helped an unranked, unseeded local boy named Adriano Panatta make it all the way to the finals in 1978. Through sheer bedlam, the crazed fans threw his opponents off their game, making them double fault and hit unforced errors. With the crowd as his doubles partner, Panatta beat the best Americans in the tournament—Vitas Gerulaitis, Terry Moor, Hank Pfister, and Victor Amaya.

The fans' most shameful triumph came in the semifinals when Panatta faced José Higueras of Spain. Higueras looked unbeatable as he won the first nine games and held a commanding 5–1 lead in the second set. That's when the stunned crowd woke up and went to work. With Italians screaming, yelling, and taunting the Spaniard, Panatta saved four set points in the next three games to make it 4–5.

At set point in the next game, Panatta returned a volley with a weak lob that Higueras figured to kill with an easy overhead smash. But as the ball descended, the crowd raised the decibel level of their shrieking. And the simple shot that should have given Higueras the set went into the net.

Amid howls of derision from the mob, the Spaniard slapped his hand over the inside of his elbow with his fist thrust upward. No translation was needed. The crowd went wild with outrage. The punks in the cheap upper seats hurled beer cans and coins at Higueras, who stalked off the court and threatened to quit. After five minutes of pleading from officials, Higueras reluctantly returned to the court.

On the next point, the ball was still in play when someone threw a 100-lire coin (about the size of a 50-cent piece) that hit the Spaniard on the foot just as Panatta was winning the point. This clearly was interference, but the mob had so intimidated the officials that they remained mum. Higueras lost his serve and Panatta won his with ease. During the changeover at 5–6, Higueras again tried to escape the madhouse, but was coaxed back onto the court by the Davis Cup captain of Spain. However, the taunting crowd made so much noise, refusing to be silenced, that umpire Bertie Bowron of England got out of his chair and walked off. Higueras then deliberately knocked four balls into the net to lose the set, picked up his racquets, and left. Panatta—and the crowd—won the match, 0–6, 7–5, default.

"Even after Bertie left the chair, I still wanted to play," said Higueras after the match. "But when I heard myself being called a cretin and a son of a bitch, I realized that with my state of mind, I could not continue the match."

Although the fans helped Panatta make the finals, they couldn't help him win it. Not when his opponent was Bjorn Borg, then the world's best player and known for his coolness under fire. During the finals, the crowd hurled taunts, coins, and telephone slugs at Borg, but true to form, the Swede just picked up the coins, gave them to the umpire, and went on to win the championship.

"I was very irritated with the crowd," Borg said later. "If they had thrown a few more coins, I would have quit." Then in a final observation that no one would deny, he added, "The center court in Rome is the most difficult place in the world to win against an Italian."

Dorothy Cavis-Brown

Lineswoman ■ Wimbledon ■ June 22, 1964

Imagine waking up from a nice snooze, stretching, and expecting to see the light streaming in from your bedroom window. Instead, you bolt up and, with a sickening feeling in the pit of your stomach, realize that you're on a Wimbledon court where two tennis players and thousands of fans are pointing and laughing at you.

Such an incredibly embarrassing moment befell Dorothy Cavis-Brown, a lineswoman who actually fell asleep in—of all places—the middle of a match at the oldest and most prestigious tennis tournament in the world.

Dorothy, one of the most respected lineswomen in England at the time, was responsible for watching one of the sidelines during a

1964 Wimbledon match between American Clark Graebner and South African Abe Segal. Staring at a line got so downright boring that she fell asleep on the job in the final set. At first, all eyes were on the tennis action; no one noticed the prim and proper Englishwoman as she dozed and tilted to one side in her chair.

Graebner, who wound up losing in straight sets, didn't realize the lineswoman was slumbering until Segal hit a shot wide of the line and Dorothy didn't call it "out." In fact, Dorothy didn't call it anything. Instead of 40-love, it was forty winks. "I noticed that she was slumped over slightly, head down," Graebner recalled. "I went over and nudged her. Frankly, it was to see if she had died. Well, she bobbed her head slightly, but she didn't wake up. Eventually she did, but by then everyone had noticed her dozing. In the stands there was quite a lot of uproarious laughter, at least by British standards."

Chagrined officials at the All England Club decided it was best if Dorothy took a couple of days off from the tournament to catch up on her sleep. She was rarely seen at the club again. Some said Dorothy was spending most of her time in the land of Nod.

Dorothy in Wimbledon nightmare   AP/Wide World Photos

Earl Cochell

U.S. Nationals ■ August 29, 1951

John McEnroe and Jimmy Connors may be the bad boys of tennis, but they can't hold a candle to Earl Cochell. His hot temper got him banned from tennis for *life*.

The tennis establishment didn't take kindly to his obscenity-laced, on-the-court rantings. But what finally did Cochell in was the time he stormed the umpire's chair, climbed up, and tried to wrest control of the official's microphone to cuss out the crowd at the U.S. Nationals.

Cochell, a stocky, feisty Californian with a big serve and an even bigger temper, was ranked among the top ten players from 1947 to 1951. But his career came to an abrupt and fiery end at the 1951 U.S. Nationals in Forest Hills, New York. After the 29-year-old player breezed through the first three rounds, he faced Gardnar Mulloy. The pair split the first two sets before the volatile Cochell exploded.

Behind 3–1 in the third set, Cochell screamed in rage over a close call that went against him. The crowd booed him and, in response, he shouted at the fans to shut up—which, of course, they wouldn't do. Then he decided to throw the game by switching his racquet to his left hand and feebly returning Mulloy's serves. Naturally, Cochell lost the game. Down 4–1, he deliberately tossed away the next game by using soft underhand serves.

By now the crowd hooted and jeered Cochell so loudly that he stopped play, shook his racquet at the gallery, cursed them loudly, and then decided to commandeer the umpire's microphone. Recalled

Mulloy, "He went to the chair and started climbing up to get the microphone. The umpire tried to shove him off, the two of them struggling up there over the mike like a pair of bears in the top of a tree, their voices bouncing out over the open mike: 'Go on, get out of here,' 'Lemme talk to those SOBs,' that sort of thing." Amid a chorus of more boos, Cochell returned to the court and threw the seventh game to lose the set 6–1.

A ten-minute break followed three split sets. In the dressing room beneath the stadium, tournament referee Dr. S. Ellsworth Davenport, a gentle, elderly man, tried to lecture Cochell on his behavior but never got the chance. Cochell blasted him with a barrage of vile language unheard of back then at the tennis club.

Cochell returned to the court where he played listlessly but without further incident and lost the fourth set and the match 4–6, 6–2, 6–1, 6–2.

Two days later, Cochell discovered that he had lost much more than just the match. The executive committee of the United States Lawn Tennis Association banned Cochell for "unsportsmanlike conduct on the court and related actions detrimental to the welfare of the game."

After receiving this punishment, Cochell vanished.

Stallers and Bawlers

Bad Boys Notorious for Delaying Games

• Frank Kovacs. Played in the 1930s and '40s. Often stopped play to complain about the heavy nap on the balls. Protested by shoving a ball in his teeth and gnawing away at the nap.

• Wayne Sabin. Played in the 1930s and '40s. Used to angrily throw his racquet high into the seats so he could rest during the time it took the ball boys to fetch it.

• Bobby Riggs. Habitually tongue-lashed linesmen about their calls—even though he knew they were correct—just to catch a breather.

• Ilie Nastase. The Mad Romanian. Expert at stopping play by deliberately hitting balls at linesmen, harassing photographers, and inciting fans with obscene gestures.

• John McEnroe. Superbrat. One of the all-time great stallers, he perfected the art of buying time by constantly tying his shoelaces (a record seven times during one 1979 Wimbledon match). Also known for deliberately breaking his racquet.

THE BASEBALL
HALL OF SHAME
THE NEWEST INDUCTEES

Norm McMillan's Inside-the-Jacket Grand Slam Homer

August 26, 1929

Of all the grand slammers ever clubbed, none was more undeserving than the one swatted by Norm McMillan. That's because Lady Luck had something up her sleeve.

The Chicago Cubs and the visiting Cincinnati Reds were tied 5–5 in the bottom of the eighth inning at Wrigley Field when McMillan, the Cubs' third baseman, stepped up to the plate with the bases loaded.

McMillan bounced a base hit over the third base bag for what looked like a two-run double. The ball rolled toward the Chicago bull pen, located in foul territory along the left-field line, where the Cubs' relief corps scattered to get out of the way. Cincy's rookie left fielder Evar Swanson raced over to where he thought the ball should be. But it was nowhere in sight.

While the Chicago runners gleefully scampered around the bases, Swanson frantically searched over, under, and around the bull pen bench. He still couldn't find the ball. By the time McMillan had crossed home with a grand slam, Swanson was fit to be tied. He grabbed Cub relief pitcher Ken Penner's warmup jacket, which had been lying underneath the bench, and hurled it to the ground in disgust. The ball rolled out of the jacket sleeve!

McMillan's cheap inside-the-jacket home run was the only grand slammer of his career and it won the game, 9–5.

What was the "wildest" ending to a World Series?

When Pittsburgh Pirates' hurler John Miljus threw a wild pitch in the ninth inning of Game Four of the 1927 Series. With the score tied 3–3 and the bases loaded for the New York Yankees, Miljus uncorked an errant pitch with Tony Lazzeri at bat. Runner Earle Combs trotted home with the winning run as the Yankees defeated the Pirates 4–3 and swept the Series.

Ron "Rocky" Swoboda

Outfielder ■ New York, N.L. ■ May 23, 1965

Ron Swoboda's temper tantrum was so pitiful that he was ejected from the game—by his own manager!

Swoboda, then a 20-year-old rookie with the New York Mets, was playing right field against the Cardinals in St. Louis on a day with intermittent rain. Although the Mets were leading 7–2 in the bottom of the ninth, the team credo was "The game is never over until the final error." The Cardinals rallied for two runs and had the bases loaded. However, they were down to their last out with Dal Maxvill, a .135 hitter, at the plate.

Rocky between temper tantrums   AP/Wide World Photos

"Just then the sun popped through the clouds," recalled Swoboda. "We'd had so many rain delays that when I went out to right field for the ninth, I forgot my sunglasses. The prudent thing would have been to call time and go get them. But that would have been embarrassing to me. Of course, what happened next was much more embarrassing.

"Maxvill hit a dying quail in front of me and I lost it in the sun. The ball got by me for a three-run triple and the Cards tied the score."

At the end of the inning, Swoboda ran into the dugout and began cussing himself out over his horrendous misplay. As the second hitter in the top of the tenth, Ron was determined to atone for his gaffe. Unfortunately, he could do no better than duplicate Maxvill's batting performance—another dying quail to, of all places, right field. The only difference was that this one was easily caught.

"We went three up and three down and I was still in a serious state of pissivity," Swoboda recounted. "As I headed up the dugout steps to take my position in right, I saw my batting helmet upside down on the ground. So I jumped on it in anger. But it didn't break. Instead, I got my foot caught in it.

"There I was out in front of the dugout, hopping on one foot, trying to get the helmet off my spikes when out came [manager] Casey Stengel. He grabbed me by the shirt and kicked me in the rear and yelled, 'God damn it! When you popped out to right, I didn't run into the clubhouse and throw your watch on the floor and jump on it, so I don't want you busting up the team's equipment!'

"I started to run out to right field, still trying to shake the damn helmet off my foot. I know I must have looked like a one hundred percent fool out there. Casey yelled at me to come back and then he threw me out of the game.

"The Cardinals went on to win in the thirteenth inning. It was all my fault. I was totally out of control and Casey did the right thing when he jerked my ass out of the game. I went into the clubhouse and cried. It seemed like the only thing to do."

San Francisco Giants

June 26–29, 1961

Manager Alvin Dark could have sued the San Francisco Giants for mental cruelty after what his team did to him.

During a five-game series with the last-place Philadelphia Phillies, the visiting second-place Giants tortured their skipper with plays so horrifying they belonged in a Stephen King novel. Two of the plays—which no one recalled ever seeing before—gave rise to the theory that the team had held its spring training in hell.

In the series opener, San Francisco's appalling performance drove the usually mild-mannered Dark to lose more than just his mind—he lost part of his finger as well. Trailing 1–0 in the seventh inning, the Giants put runners on second and third with no outs, but came up empty after three straight infield grounders. In the eighth, San Francisco again had runners at second and third, this time with one out, and failed to score. Then in the ninth, the team had runners on the corners with one out, but couldn't push across the tying tally. The Giants lost 1–0.

Dark's blood not only boiled, it spilled. Enraged at the impotence of his troops, the frustrated manager stormed into the clubhouse after the game's last out, snatched a metal stool, and hurled it across the room. Part of the little finger of his right hand went with it when his finger tip was sliced off on a jagged edge of the stool. He was rushed to the hospital where his wounded digit—minus the tip—was stitched up.

The players felt bad for causing Dark such anguish, so they decided to give him a peace offering. They found the tip of his little finger and pickled it in a jar of alcohol. Then they presented it to Dark before the next game. "There wasn't much I could say except thank you," recalled Dark. "I vowed that I wouldn't take my anger out on myself anymore."

It was a good thing, too, or else Dark would have slit his throat after what happened in the third game of the series. The Phillies had battled the Giants to a 4–4 tie entering the fifteenth inning of a night game when the umpires told both dugouts that this would be the final inning because of a curfew law. San Francisco then quickly erupted for three runs in the top of the frame and Dark relaxed, thinking that victory was cinched.

But moments later, the Giants saddled their manager with untold grief and aggravation by allowing Philadelphia to rally for two runs. The Phils had the tying and winning runs at third and first, and were down to their final out. It was all up to batter Clay Dalrymple. On the first pitch, hurler Mike McCormick fired a strike past him. Then came an astoundingly exasperating play that would have put most managers in a straitjacket. Giants' catcher Hobie Landrith flipped the ball back to McCormick too hard and the ball sailed over the pitcher's head into short center field. Before the ball could be retrieved by any of Landrith's shocked teammates, Phils runner Tony Gonzalez happily scampered home from third with the tying run.

With the restraint of a saint, Dark dug his fingers into the bench and bit his tongue in silent agony. On the next pitch, Dalrymple grounded out. After five hours and eleven minutes, the game ended at 1:15 A.M. tied at 7–7. "I didn't do anything or say anything," recalled Dark. "I was afraid of what might happen if I did either."

The Giants weren't through vexing their manager. They made his flesh crawl the next day with a play almost as appalling as Landrith's blunder. In the bottom of the first inning, the Phillies had tied the score at 2–2 and had runners Tony Gonzalez and Don Demeter at first and second, respectively, with one out. Clay Dalrymple—the same batter who was at the plate in San Francisco's previous nightmare—hit what looked like a second-to-short-to-first inning-ending double play. However, umpire Ed Sudol had called Gonzalez safe at second. But the Giants infielders were so sure they had pulled off the twin killing that they trotted toward the dugout as first baseman Willie McCovey rolled the ball to the pitcher's mound. Meanwhile, Demeter and Gonzalez continued to race around the bases and scored two unchallenged runs before the San Francisco outfielders, who were jogging off the field, could react.

No one would have blamed Dark for losing his temper. Somehow, he managed to keep his composure. "We won that game and the series," he said, "but I almost didn't survive it."

Well, Exc-u-u-u-se Me!

Wacky Diamond Cop-outs

Philadelphia Athletics runner Jimmy Dykes, when asked why he didn't slide into second, 1925:

"I couldn't. I carry my cigars in my back pocket and I was afraid I'd break them."

Kansas City Royals outfielder Clint Hurdle, explaining why he misplayed a fly ball, 1981:

"I was playing it like [All-Star teammate] Willie Wilson, but I forgot that I'm in Clint Hurdle's body."

Los Angeles Angels pitcher Bo Belinsky, trying to excuse his poor pitching in a 15–0 rout, 1963:

"How can a guy win a game if you don't give him any runs?"

Los Angeles Dodgers outfielder Reggie Smith, explaining why he didn't leap for a home run ball, 1978:

"Why should I go jackknifing over the fence on my head? That ball has got no business being out there four hundred feet."

San Francisco Giants pitcher Billy Loes, when asked why he never won twenty games in a season, 1961:

"Oh, hell, if you win twenty games, they want you to do it every year."

Philadelphia Phillies manager Gene Mauch, explaining why he waited so long before pulling a pitcher who was getting bombed, 1965:

"I was afraid I might strangle him if I had him in the dugout."

Sammy White

Catcher ■ Boston, A.L. ■ August 28, 1956

Enraged over an umpire's decision, Boston Red Sox catcher Sammy White tried to show up the arbiter. So White defiantly hurled the ball into deep center field. He stood proudly over this act of rebellion— until he suddenly realized that the ball he had thrown was still in play.

Then White stood mortified as the runner on first trotted around the bases and scored.

Sammy's witless outburst flared up in the top of the sixth inning at Fenway Park with the Detroit Tigers leading the Red Sox, 3–0. Bill Tuttle was on second base when Red Wilson slapped an infield hit. Tuttle sped around third and, without stopping, dashed for home. Shortstop Milt Bolling pegged the ball to White at the plate, but umpire Frank Umont called Tuttle safe.

Sammy blew a fuse. Flinging his mask off, he charged after the ump and cursed him. Then, in a final act of disgust for all to see, White heaved the ball into center field. This was not a wise thing to do for three reasons: No. 1, the ball was still in play; No. 2, center-fielder Jimmy Piersall had trotted in to second base and was standing there with the infielders watching White's tirade; No. 3, Umont had just given White the boot.

Since the ball remained unattended in the outfield grass, Red Wilson took off for second. As Wilson rounded the bag and headed for third, left fielder Ted Williams finally retrieved the ball and tossed it back into the infield.

Meanwhile, White and Bosox manager Pinky Higgins were carrying on a diatribe with Umont, so Detroit's third base coach Billy Hitchcock waved Wilson around third. The Red Sox infielders helplessly watched Wilson score unmolested because White had his back turned to them and was out of position.

Higgins protested the game, claiming that time was automatically called the second Umont ejected White. But the umpire declared, "White was not thrown out of the game until he threw the ball. When he threw the ball, he put it in play and we couldn't call time until the play was finished. And it didn't finish until Wilson crossed the plate."

The Red Sox lost not only the game, 6–3, but the protest as well. As for White, he lost some pride and fifty dollars from a fine levied by the league office.

Mel Hall

Outfielder ■ Cleveland, A.L. ■ March 16, 1986

Leftfielder Mel Hall became so caught up in a spring training game that he hung his head—and uniform—in shame.

In the fourth inning of the Cleveland Indians' game against the Oakland A's in Phoenix, A's batter Carney Lansford hit a looping line drive over third base. Hall chased the ball into foul territory near a restraining fence that separated the field from the bleachers.

Suddenly, Hall was stopped dead in his tracks as though he had been caught in a stop-action video replay. The fence had snared the long-sleeved T-shirt under his jersey. Hall couldn't move and was forced to watch helplessly as the ball bounced merrily away from him.

Shortstop Julio Franco raced out to retrieve the ball, but when he realized that Hall was all hung up, Franco could do nothing but laugh hysterically. Meanwhile, Lansford circled the bases for an inside-the-park home run.

Hall was still trying to free himself when his manager, Pat Corrales, began arguing with umpire Don Denkinger that the ball was foul. Mused Oakland manager Jackie Moore, "This is the first time I can remember a discussion about whether a player, rather than the ball, was in play."

After Hall unsnagged himself, teammate Joe Carter had a suggestion: "Mel needs a tear-away jersey."

With eight .300 hitters on his 1930 team, why did Philadelphia Phillies manager Burt Shotton climb the clubhouse walls in frustration?

The Phils finished last, forty games out of first with a deplorable 52–102 record. They could hit; they just couldn't pitch or field. The club made 239 errors and posted a whopping 6.71 ERA—a major league pitching mark that still stands.

Ed "Whitey" Appleton

Pitcher ■ Brooklyn Dodgers ■ August 7, 1915

In a line of nice guys who finished last, Ed Appleton brought up the rear.

In one unforgettable game, the rookie pitcher for the Brooklyn Dodgers was so obliging and polite that he did exactly as he was told—by the opposing manager. And when the crafty skipper asked Appleton to throw the game away, he did just that.

Pitching in the bottom of the seventh inning against the St. Louis Cardinals, Appleton found himself in a jam. With the score tied 4–4, the Cards loaded the bases with two out. The pressure was building.

St. Louis manager Miller Huggins thought it was the perfect time to try to con the tense young hurler. Coaching at third base, Huggins yelled to the mound, "Hey, Appleton! Lessee that old ball!"

Appleton had been raised to be polite and respectful toward his elders. Apparently he wasn't raised to be very smart. Willing to accommodate so distinguished a baseball man as Miller Huggins, Appleton turned toward the coaching box and tossed him the ball before any of the disbelieving Brooklyn infielders could do a thing. As the ball floated through the air, a grinning Huggins nimbly stepped aside and watched it bound toward the third base box seats. By the time the ball was retrieved, Jack Miller and Tommy Long, the runners on third and second respectively, had scampered home with the winning runs for a 6–4 victory.

"[Miller's] face was wreathed in a smile of sophistry," said an account in the *St. Louis Republic*. "Huggins, the arch perpetrator of the trick, scratched his chin and looked away from Umpire [Bill] Klem . . . Uncle Wilbert Robinson, who manages the Brooklyn outfit, seemed suddenly to have swallowed a catcher's mitt, if the fluidity of his face and his general incoherence could be taken to mean anything."

Because of Huggins's ploy, the rules were amended to prohibit a coach from acting in any manner to draw a throw by a fielder. But the rule change came much too late for the humiliated Appleton, who lasted only two years in the bigs.

"It seemed hardly less than criminal to thus forever wreck this guileless youth's confidence in diamond nature," said the *Republic*. "But professional baseball is professional baseball with about as much sportsmanship to it as could be squeezed through the eye of a needle."

Bob Elliott   Bobby Hofman

Third Baseman ■ **New York, N.L.** ■ **Pinch Hitter**
August 23, 1952

In the most shameful double-barreled ejection in baseball history, a hitter was thumbed out of the game *before* finishing his turn at bat—and afterward so was his pinch hitter.

The visiting New York Giants were trailing the St. Louis Cardinals 3–0 in the top of the seventh inning when Bob Elliott stepped to the plate. Plate umpire Augie Donatelli called the first pitch a strike and Elliott squawked in protest. When the next pitch was called a strike, he blew a gasket. Elliott launched into a tirade that he capped off by kicking dirt on the arbiter.

Donatelli wasted no time in banishing Elliott from the game. But the hotheaded player refused to leave. Instead he tried to get at Donatelli's throat and had to be restrained by the other three umps. His coaches finally managed to hustle him off to the showers to cool off.

Meanwhile, Bobby Hofman was sent up to the plate to finish Elliott's turn at bat with the count 0 and 2. Hofman mumbled something unfriendly to Donatelli and then settled into the batter's box. He took the next pitch and then heard Donatelli bellow out, "Steeeriiike threeee!"

That was Hofman's cue to reprise Elliott's hopping-mad performance. After venting his spleen, he, too, kicked dirt on the ump and was promptly thumbed out of the game.

For Elliott and Hofman, it was one, two, three strikes, you're kicked out of the old ball game.

(Under)wear and Tear

Like many ballplayers, Toronto Blue Jays catcher Rick Cerone was superstitious. Unlike his colleagues, he had one of the weirdest good luck charms ever—his long underwear.

When the 1979 season began, Cerone decided to don long johns under his uniform because it was so chilly in April. Because he got off to a fast start at the plate, the superstitious catcher continued to wear the longies for every game. That was fine when the weather was cool. But by the dog days of summer, the only luck his long johns brought him was bad. Heavy from sweat, the hot longies slowed down Cerone, but he refused to put them away. As a result, the pitchers put him away with regularity and Cerone finished the year with a lowly batting average of .239.

Leo Foster

Shortstop ■ Atlanta, N.L. ■ July 9, 1971

Leo Foster deserved a standing boo for his performance in his very first major league game. He was responsible for five of his team's outs in just two at-bats.

Called up by the Atlanta Braves because four regulars were fulfilling their military obligations as weekend warriors, Foster was penciled into the starting lineup for a game against the Pirates in Pittsburgh.

The big leagues proved tougher than Leo ever imagined. He didn't get off to a good start, making an error on the very first ball ever hit to him. It happened in the bottom of the first inning when he muffed a routine grounder tapped by lead-off batter Dave Cash. Moments later, Cash scored the game's first run.

Foster had even worse luck at the plate. In the fifth inning, Leo batted with two men on and one out. But he hit into a rally-killing double play. Those things happen to the best of players. However, most players go through their entire careers without suffering the kind of ignobility that Foster experienced in his next plate appearance.

In the seventh inning, the Braves threatened once again with runners on first and second and no outs. Leo stepped into the batter's box. Here was his chance to atone for his first-inning error and his inning-ending double play. Here was his chance to make a name for himself. Here was his chance to prove that he belonged in the bigs.

Leo whacked a grounder to Richie Hebner at third base. Hebner stepped on the bag to force the runner coming from second, and then fired the ball to Dave Cash at second. Cash took the throw, stepped on the base for the force-out of the runner from first, and then pivoted and pegged the ball to Bob Robertson at first. The throw was just in time to nip Foster.

Poor Leo. He had just hit into the league's first triple play of the season. After the game, won by the Pirates 11–2, Foster admitted that his debut "wasn't exactly what I thought it would be."

Who did Ken Johnson have to blame for becoming the only pitcher ever to lose a nine-inning complete-game no-hitter?

Himself. On April 23, 1964, the Houston Colt pitcher silenced the bats of the Cincinnati Reds. But in the ninth inning of a 0–0 tie, Johnson fielded Pete Rose's bunt and threw wildly to first allowing Rose to reach second. Rose moved to third on a groundout and scored the only run of the game on another error.

Chicken Wolf's Homer

August 22, 1886

A player named Chicken Wolf hit a homer that could only be called a dog-gone shame.

He needed the help of a snarling canine to beat the Cincinnati Reds with a game-winning four-bagger.

The visiting Reds had battled the Louisville Colonels to a 3–3 tie when Wolf, the Colonels' rightfielder, stepped to the plate in the bottom of the tenth inning. All eyes were on Wolf, who had already smacked a game-tying homer in the ninth. No eyes were on the curled-up, mangy mongrel dozing at the base of the center-field fence.

That would soon change. Chicken Wolf slammed a drive to deep center field. With the crack of the bat, Reds outfielder Abner Powell took off—and so did the suddenly awakened dog. The mutt reached Powell before the outfielder reached the ball.

Like a hound after a mailman, the dog clamped its iron jaws shut on Powell's pants just below the back of the knee and wouldn't let go. While Wolf galloped around the bases, Powell tried to shake himself free, and then in desperation, he started hopping toward the ball, dragging the dog behind him. Not until Wolf crossed home plate with the game-winning, inside-the-park home run did Powell break the mutt's grip. Poor Powell—remembered after a century only for dogging it in the outfield.

Rusty Staub

First Baseman ■ Houston, N.L. ■ May 17, 1968

Rusty Staub was the only first baseman ever caught and punished for an illegal *pitch*. A spitball, no less.

The Houston Astros were losing 4–0 to the Los Angeles Dodgers in the bottom of the eighth inning at Dodger Stadium when Rusty was caught wet-handed. Houston starter Larry Dierker, who had struggled all night, had just given up his eleventh hit, a single to Paul Popovich.

When Dierker ran the count to 3 and 0 against the next batter, opposing pitcher Bill Singer, Staub called time and strolled from his first base position to the mound. Dierker flipped him the ball to rub up while Rusty tried to boost his pitcher's confidence. "C'mon, you can get him out," said Staub. "He's going to take your pitches. Don't walk him."

Dierker didn't. But Rusty unthinkingly did. As he talked with the pitcher, Staub spit on the ball. No player can do that legally while standing on the pitching mound. Rusty forgot that rule but the umpires didn't. They immediately called an automatic ball on the batter—even though no pitch was actually thrown. So Singer drew a walk.

The now-nettled Dierker walked the next batter—the conventional way—before he was sent to the showers. The Astros went on to lose 6–0. After that episode, Houston pitchers wouldn't let Staub so much as touch the ball during conferences on the mound.

All-Time Hall of Shame Names

Bow Wow Arft, 1B, 1948–52
Creepy Crespi, 2B, 1938–42
Yo Yo Davalillo, SS, 1953
Piano Legs Hickman, 3B, 1897–1908
Ding-a-Ling Clay, OF, 1943–46
Peek-a-Boo Veach, OF, 1884–87
Tomato Face Cullop, OF, 1926–31
Dodo Bird, C, 1892
Heinie Meine, P, 1929–34

New York Mets

September 22, 1965

The New York Mets should have hired a booking agent and taken their most outrageous fielding performance on the road. It wasn't baseball; it was slapstick comedy.

Maintaining their early image as the clowns of the game, the Mets turned an ordinary single into a four-run, three-error play that left the disbelieving crowd weak from laughter.

The Mets were losing to the Pirates 2–1 in the bottom of the fifth inning when Pittsburgh loaded the bases with one out and Donn Clendenon at the plate. When Clendenon stroked a liner through pitcher Tug McGraw's legs and into center field, the fun began.

Centerfielder Jim Hickman came charging in, bent down, and scooped up nothing but air. The ball shot right past him and rolled to the deepest part of the outfield. The runners on second and third scored easily on the error as Roberto Clemente, the runner on first, and Clendenon tore around the bases. Hickman retrieved the ball and fired it to shortstop Buddy Harrelson, the cutoff man. Harrelson tried to gun down Clemente at third, but his relay was wild and bounced off the glove of leaping third baseman Charley Smith. Thankful for the back-to-back errors, Clemente darted for home.

Meanwhile, McGraw scrambled after the ball and took his shot at nailing Clemente at the plate. Tug nailed the on-deck circle instead as the throw sailed over the head of catcher Greg Goossen. Clemente scored the third run of the play on the Mets' third error. By now, Goossen had abandoned his post at home to flag down the ball.

McGraw raced to the plate to cover home, hoping to nab the only Pirate runner who hadn't scored on the play yet—Clendenon, the batter who hit the ball in the first place. Goossen finally picked up the ball and threw it to Tug, who whirled around and tagged Clendenon. But it was too late.

The Mets had staged a hilarious farce—three errors and four runs on one screwed-up play. At least the Mets did see one player thrown out. Unfortunately, it was McGraw.

Looking like a permanent resident of the loony bin, Tug irately jumped up and down, cursing himself and his teammates after the "grand slam." But as luck would have it, home plate umpire Al Forman was standing right next to the sorehead and assumed that

Tug, with good reason to curse AP/Wide World Photos

McGraw's invectives were directed at him. So Forman gave Tug the old heave-ho.

As the fuming pitcher stalked toward the clubhouse, he had to pass through the Pirates dugout, where he received an earful of razzing. "Hey, Tug," said Clendenon. "Who were you cussing?"

"I was cussing, but I didn't mean him," replied McGraw, pointing to the umpire.

"Then who did you mean?"

McGraw, still hot under the collar, glowered at Clendenon and snarled, "You, you son of a bitch!"

Can't Anybody Here Play This Game?

In a 1974 game against the Chicago White Sox, the Minnesota Twins refined the art of Metsian diamond debacles.

With two outs, Chicago runners Dick Allen and Ken Henderson were on second and first, respectively, while batter Ron Santo worked the count to 3-and-2. As both runners broke with the pitch, Santo took a half-swing. Home plate umpire Marty Springstead delayed his call to check with the first base ump over whether Santo had swung or not. Meanwhile, Twins catcher Randy Hundley, thinking the count was 2-and-2, threw to third trying to nail Allen. But Twins third baseman Eric Soderholm, who thought Santo had struck out, was trotting off the field. The ball sailed into left field and Allen scored.

Adding to their misery, Minnesota pitcher Ray Corbin rushed umpire Springstead to protest the play and accidentally shoved Hundley, who reinjured his knee and was rendered virtually useless for the rest of the season.

Then, and only then, did everyone learn that Santo had indeed struck out to end the inning.

THE FOOTBALL
HALL OF SHAME
THE NEWEST INDUCTEES

Bill Cosby

Alumnus ■ **Temple University** ■ **November 30, 1984**

Bill Cosby—yes, *the* Bill Cosby—should have been flagged for intentional grounding.

Right in the middle of a collegiate football game, the superstar comedian sneaked out onto the field, swiped an official's flag, and buried it under the turf. When Cosby was ordered to find it, he tried, but to no avail.

Cosby was part of the grounds crew on the sideline of a game between his alma mater, Temple, and the University of Toledo at the Atlantic City, New Jersey, Convention Center. The non-conference clash was played indoors as part of a weekend celebration honoring Temple's one hundredth anniversary. The arena, site of the Miss America pageant, was groomed for football by laying pieces of sod over the cement floor. However, the game was frequently delayed to relocate displaced sod that had been kicked up during the action. Cosby and the other groundsmen had to run out onto the field and tamp down the loose sod when necessary.

In the third quarter, referee Larry Glass threw his penalty flag when a Toledo player ran into the Temple punter. That was when Cosby, decked out in a Temple sweatshirt, decided to have some fun at the ref's expense.

Unbeknownst to Glass, Cosby sneaked onto the field, took the flag and buried it under a piece of sod. After Glass gave the signal for running into the kicker, talked to the team captain, and marked off the penalty, he walked back to the area where he had thrown the flag. But he couldn't find it. According to Glass, here's what happened next:

One of the players told Glass, "Cosby buried your flag under one of those pieces of sod."

So, while holding up the game, Glass marched over to Cosby on the sideline and said, "Where's my flag?"

"Can you finish the game without it?" asked Cosby.

"Hell no, you son of a bitch! I need the flag. Get it now!"

"I know right where it's at." Cosby *thought* he knew where it was. But as the players waited, he and some other members of the grounds crew pulled up a dozen pieces of sod and couldn't find the hidden flag. "Oh, well, it's under there somewhere," Cosby told Glass. "We'll find it."

"What am I supposed to do between now and the end of the game?" asked Glass. Just then another ref who had brought along an extra flag walked over to Glass and gave it to him. Meanwhile, the Toledo coaches were demanding that the ref penalize Temple for the Cosby-caused delay. The ref refused.

After the game (won by Temple 35–6), Cosby told Glass, "I'll see that you get the flag. We're going to take up all the sod tomorrow and I'll be there and get it. Then I'll autograph it and send it to you."

Glass claims he never did get his flag back and is still ticked off at Cosby. "To this day," said the ref, "I won't watch his TV show."

Cosby in search of the lost flag   Temple University

Spitting Image

The Penn State Nittany Lions went undefeated in 1912 due in part to their linemen's special talent—spitting.

To show everyone how tough they were, the Nittany Lions played with big wads of tobacco jammed in their cheeks. But their chaws were more than just their trademark; they were their weapons. Throughout the season, the linemen sprayed their opponents with tobacco juice.

Campbell Graf, a star on the Ohio State Buckeyes who played against the 8–0 Nittany Lions in 1912, later recalled that the Penn State tobacco spitters "were both powerful and accurate—they blinded us most of the afternoon by using our eyes as targets."

Rick Eber

Wide Receiver ■ Shreveport Steamer ■ 1974

Rick Eber was the tackiest receiver in pro football. He caught passes that others would have dropped because he taped thumbtacks to his fingertips!

Eber illegally sharpened his receiving skills for the Shreveport Steamer of the short-lived World Football League. "Those WFL refs were something else," he said. "I'd catch a ball and give it back to them with scratches all over it and they never suspected a thing."

Revealing his secret exclusively for *The Sports Hall of SHAME*, Eber explained, "I cut the tacks down until there were just little nubs left on them. Then I taped them to my fingers and covered them with shoe polish. You can really hold onto the football that way and yet the tacks are short enough so that you won't puncture yourself or the ball."

Eber said he used the thumbtacks for several games, as did some of his teammates, who learned the trick from him. "One of our receivers didn't have great hands, so I showed him how to use the thumbtacks. He looked terrific. One time, right in the middle of a rain storm, he leaped for a pass and, with those thumbtacks, caught the *tail end* of the ball as it went by him. He came back to the huddle and told me, 'Man, I'm gonna wear these tacks every day!' "

Thanks to the tacks, Eber really stuck it to his defenders during an away game against the Philadelphia Bell. Despite playing on a muddy field in a driving rain with a slippery ball, Eber snared five receptions, including two for touchdowns in the first half.

"I broke some of the tacks and wore down the others, so at halftime I put on new tacks in the locker room. The towel guy saw me do it. I didn't know he was being paid by the Bell. At the start of the third quarter, he went over to the other side and squealed on me to the Philadelphia coach, who then told an official. The ref asked to see my hands. So I showed them to him—palms down. He just said okay and walked away. That shows you how bright the referees were in the WFL. Then he came back a few minutes later and said, 'Let me see your hands again. Only this time turn them over.' When I did, he rolled his eyes and said, 'I don't believe this!' He made me go to the sideline and take the tacks off. If the refs had bothered to check, they would have found three of my teammates guilty as well. While I was being examined, the other guys were in the huddle with their hands behind their backs, unwrapping the tacks as quickly as they could."

After Eber took his tacks off, he dropped everything that was thrown his way and never did catch another pass the rest of the game. Fortunately for the Steamer, Eber was nailed after he already had hauled in the winning touchdown.

"The refs would have found me out sooner or later," he said. "They would have said, 'Why is it that every time you catch a football and hand it back to us, it's leaking air?'"

Eber revealing his tacky secret   Ron Eisenberg Photo

Chicago Cardinals vs. Detroit Lions

September 15, 1940

It was the worst pro football game ever played.

From an offensive point of view, it was exactly that—offensive. The Chicago Cardinals and the Detroit Lions bored each other to death in a 0–0 tie that set an NFL record for futility. The two teams gained an incredibly paltry total of thirty combined yards from scrimmage the entire game; sixteen for the Lions and fourteen for the Cardinals. Even the neighborhood seamstress chalks up more yardage than that on a Sunday afternoon.

The teams utterly failed to muster anything remotely resembling an offense. They couldn't have made any points with a pencil sharpener. They played as if the game was dedicated to insomniacs. The lousy weather, not the game, kept awake the 18,000 fans who witnessed this dreadful, scoreless deadlock at War Memorial Stadium in Buffalo, which occasionally played host to an NFL game back then.

Shortly after the opening kickoff, a blinding, chilly rainstorm turned the field into a muddy quagmire fit for hog heaven. As was typical in those days, the teams played the whole game with the same ball. There was no towel to dry it off between plays, so the pigskin turned into a heavy oblong mass of mud.

"The mud kept getting into our faces," recalled Detroit's All-Pro center and linebacker Alex Wojciechowicz. "The worst aspect of the game was the fact that our hands kept getting burned by the lime that was formed by the combination of rain mixing with the dirt in the field. We all had to get treated for burns at some time during the game."

Because neither team carried a spare set of jerseys, the players soon became nameless blobs. "You couldn't read any of the numbers on the uniforms and you couldn't distinguish the colors of the uniforms," said Wojciechowicz. "Everyone looked exactly the same—awful."

In spite of the horrendous playing conditions, the Lions almost won the game with a twenty-six-yard pass in the third quarter. It was the only completion for either team and it accounted for Detroit's total offense. Lining up in the spread formation, quarterback Dwight Sloan lobbed a wet, wobbly pass to halfback Lloyd Cardwell, who made a remarkable catch of the slippery pigskin and slogged down the field until he was tackled on the one-yard line.

Strangely, instead of tightening up his offense for a conventional plunge into the line, Sloan stayed with the spread formation. It was a bad move. Receiving the snap seven yards behind the line of scrimmage, Sloan was sacked, first for five yards and then for seven. On third-and-goal from the thirteen-yard line, he heaved a desperation pass that was intercepted.

From then on, each team went into a prevent offense. During one stretch in the fourth quarter, the teams traded eight consecutive punts without a single intervening play from scrimmage.

Chicago made only two first downs all day, tried two passes that failed, and lost one fumble. Despite rushing for minus ten yards, Detroit made five first downs. The Lions completed one of six passes and lost three fumbles.

The only time the drenched, bored fans showed any enthusiasm came after the public address announcer said, "There are only two minutes of play left." The crowd gave a standing ovation.

Gene Barth

NFL Referee ■ August 14, 1971

For his debut as an NFL referee, Gene Barth took his best shot—and hit himself in the butt.

"I started off my very first NFL game quite nervous—and quite sore," admitted Barth, now a respected veteran official.

Before taking the field to officiate a preseason game between the Denver Broncos and the visiting Washington Redskins, Barth was going over some last-minute preparations in the referees' locker room. As line judge, one of his responsibilities was firing the gun at the end of each period. So Barth made sure the pistol was loaded with blanks and then stuck it into his back pocket.

"It wasn't easy putting the gun in my pocket because I was

nervous and, besides, there wasn't much room in those football pants," Barth recalled. "When I started to withdraw my hand, one of my fingers accidentally pulled the trigger and I fired that damn gun in my pocket.

"The whole officiating crew was stunned by the loud bang. It made a hell of a noise. I was shocked, too, especially from those awful powder burns all over my rear end. I was terribly embarrassed—too embarrassed to tell the other guys that I was really hurting. I went out and officiated the game. Fortunately, in football, you don't have to sit down to officiate.

"It wasn't until I returned home that I did anything about my sore rear. I had pieces of fabric and other stuff embedded in my butt and my wife had to use a pair of tweezers to pick it all out."

Ever since then, Barth's butt-burner has been used as a lesson for new officials. Said Barth, "The veterans tell the rookie refs, 'Nothing could be worse than what happened to Gene Barth. Imagine, shooting yourself in the rear end before your very first game ever started.'"

Barth, no longer a pain in the butt   *Referee* Magazine/Jeff Nehring

Mike Freidel

Defensive Coach ■ **Augustana (S.D.) College** ■ **October 12, 1986**

As defensive coordinator for Augustana College, Mike Freidel always told his players to hit each opponent hard enough to knock him silly.

Then during one memorable game, Freidel did just that—to his team's own head coach.

It happened during the fourth quarter of Augustana's homecoming game with North Dakota. Freidel was on the sideline with head coach Jim Heinitz when Augustana recovered a crucial fumble.

"I threw up my arms like Rocky in celebration and my elbow caught Jim flush on the jaw," recalled Freidel. "He went out like a light. There he was lying flat on his back, unconscious, and what looked like a smile on his face."

While players and assistant coaches crowded around the kayoed coach, Augustana quarterback Joel Nelson rushed over. But it wasn't exactly out of concern for Heinitz's welfare. "As I started to come to," the coach said, "Joel started shaking me and said, 'Wake up! Wake up! What play do you want me to run?' "

Unconscious for about thirty seconds, Heinitz was still so woozy afterward that he let his assistants in the press box call the plays the rest of the game, won by Augustana, 19–10.

Throughout the next week, Heinitz, who nursed a sore back and a bitten tongue from the unexpected jolt, jokingly said that one of the first things he thought about doing after the elbowing was firing Freidel. "Then I figured he could stay on the staff as long as I kept him up in the press box. I wanted to avoid another cheap shot."

Adding insult to injury, his own players honored Freidel as "hitter of the week" and named Heinitz as "hittee of the week."

At the next game, Freidel, who was allowed to stay on the sidelines, discovered that his reputation had preceded him. "I found myself all alone on the sidelines," he recalled. "No one would get near me during the game. Whenever a player had to talk to me, he made sure his helmet was on and his mouth guard was in."

What was the slickest college team in the nation in 1986?
The Citadel Bulldogs. Several of its offensive linemen were caught with petroleum jelly smeared on their arms and jerseys for a game against Western Carolina. The greasy Bulldogs, who wanted to make it harder for onrushing defensive linemen to grab them, still lost 27–12.

Lamar University Cardinals

October 11, 1986

The Lamar University Cardinals were ready to kick the game-winning field goal in the closing seconds. They smartly let the clock wind down—but then stupidly forgot to call timeout! Before they could attempt the kick, the final gun sounded, signaling their defeat.

Lamar made its incredible gaffe at the end of a home game against the Northeast Louisiana Indians. After the Indians had taken a 22–21 lead late in the fourth quarter, the Cardinals drove sixty-eight yards to a fourth and goal at the one-yard line. Lamar coach Ray Alborn elected to run down the clock and take a delay of game penalty to leave Northeast with as little time as possible to come back after the kick. The coach figured the five-yard penalty would also give placekicker Mike Andrie a better angle from which to attempt the winning field goal.

With just three seconds left to play, the referees tossed a flag and assessed the Cardinals a delay of game penalty. Andrie then jogged onto the field and set up to boot the winner. But he never got the chance.

Because of a rule change implemented in 1986, Northeast had the option of having the clock restarted after the penalty. Naturally, the Indians took that option. All Lamar had to do was then call timeout. But the Cardinals were still under the wrong impression that the clock didn't restart until the snap of the ball. They learned otherwise when they watched in horror as time expired.

Stunned by the 22–21 defeat that stretched their losing streak to a school record thirteen straight losses, the Cardinals wandered on the field after the game for about ten minutes, just marking time. The Indians, meanwhile, ran off the field in no time at all.

University of Vermont Catamounts

October 9, 1971

Never in the history of collegiate football has there been a more offensive—as in stinko—series of plays than those run by the University of Vermont Catamounts.

Playing at home against the University of Rhode Island Rams, the Catamounts' goal-line offensive proved so pathetic that it couldn't have scored against their marching band.

Trailing 20–16 in the fourth quarter, Vermont had a first down on the Rhode Island nine-yard line. The Catamounts gained five yards on first down, lost five on second down, and threw an incomplete pass on third down. A fourth-down pass was incomplete in the end zone, but the Rams were charged with interference, giving Vermont an automatic first-and-goal from the one-yard line.

Playing like pussy cats instead of cougars as their nickname implies, the Catamounts lost a yard, gained a yard, and threw another incomplete pass. But once again Rhode Island was flagged for interference and again Vermont had an automatic first down on the one-yard line.

Abandoning the only play that seemed to work—throwing an incomplete pass and getting an interference call—the Catamounts stayed on the ground for four straight plays. They gained two and a half feet on first down and were stacked up for no gain on the next two plays. Their sick offense was finally put out of its misery when it was stopped just an inch short of the goal line on fourth down.

The few remaining Vermont fans who had not collapsed out of sheer frustration now counted on the defense to score some points. After all, no defense would ever get a better opportunity than having their opponent backed up on its own one-inch line. But that was the problem with Vermont—no defense.

On Rhode Island's first play after taking over possession, the Rams were offside. The penalty moved the ball back half the distance to the goal, or to the half-inch line. How did the Catamounts handle this stroke of good fortune? They committed a five-yard infraction of their own, giving Rhode Island a little breathing room. From then on, the Vermont defense crumbled as the Rams drove the length of the field in a nine-play scoring drive to ice a 34–22 victory.

Summing up Vermont's incredibly shameful series, the Catamounts ran eleven plays inside the ten-yard line—including six from within the one-yard line—and failed to score. Then their equally deplorable defense tried to top that sickening performance by letting Rhode Island march ninety-nine yards, two feet, and eleven and a half inches for a touchdown.

Ricky Seeker

Center ■ Texas A & M Aggies ■ November 22, 1973

Don Shinnick

Linebacker ■ Baltimore Colts ■ November 13, 1966

War isn't the only way you can end up missing in action. Just ask Ricky Seeker and Don Shinnick. In the heat of gridiron battle, they were conspicuous by their absence.

Seeker was playing center for the Texas A & M Aggies during a home game against the arch rival Texas Longhorns. Although the Aggies were counting on their fans to help give the team an extra boost, Seeker showed his teammates that they didn't need that fabled twelfth man—they needed an eleventh man. Actually, what they needed was a center.

In the closing moments of the first half, A & M was trailing 21–7 but was threatening to score. The Aggies drove to the Texas five-yard line before a penalty pushed them back to the twenty. Out of timeouts, and with only eight seconds left on the clock, A & M had time for one more play.

A score now would not only close the gap against the highly favored Longhorns but also give a psychological lift to the underdogs going into halftime.

Above the din of a record Kyle Field crowd of 52,974, A & M quarterback David Walker called a pass play and then exhorted his teammates, "This play is gonna work!" The psyched Aggies clapped their hands as they broke the huddle and raced up to the line of scrimmage, confident they could score a last-second TD.

But then they were struck with the terrible awareness that something was not right. There was no center to snap the ball! Walker frantically looked for the missing Ricky Seeker and by the time he spotted him on the sideline, the clock had expired. The Aggies had lost a golden opportunity.

What happened to Seeker? He had thought for sure that the Aggies were attempting a field goal, so he raced off the field because another center had always snapped the ball on kicks. Unfortunately for Ricky and Texas A & M, he was wrong. Coach Emory Bellard had called for a pass. The Aggies came up short one center—and eventually twenty-nine points in a 42–13 rout.

A similar blunder occurred in the NFL when the Baltimore Colts found themselves light one man during a game against the Atlanta Falcons. With Baltimore linebacker Don Shinnick on the sidelines cheering on the offensive unit, the Colts suddenly turned the ball over on a fumble. On the next play, the Falcons ran a sweep for fifteen yards and Shinnick, still on the sidelines, shouted, "Come on, let's go! Pick it up out there! Don't let 'em run like that!" Just then one of the Colt coaches pounded Shinnick on the shoulder pads and said, "Shinnick, they just ran around *your* side. You're supposed to be in the game. We're playing a man short!"

Jerry Cramer

Safety ■ Oklahoma State University Cowboys ■ October 16, 1976

No defensive player ever went from hero to zero as quickly as Jerry Cramer.

Cramer, safety for the Oklahoma State Cowboys, was playing in a tense Big Eight Conference battle against the visiting Colorado Buffaloes. With less than a minute to go, Oklahoma State led 10–6 and needed to hold Colorado for just one more play. On fourth-and-eleven from the Cowboy eighteen-yard line, the Buffaloes' reserve quarterback Jeff Knapple lofted a desperation pass to Billy Waddy in the end zone. The ball was deflected and landed right in Cramer's hands. The 30,000 partisan Cowboy fans at Lewis Stadium rose to their feet in exultation. Victory was theirs. Or so it seemed.

All Cramer had to do was down the ball in the end zone for a touchback. Oklahoma State would then have the ball on its own twenty and could run out the clock. And Cramer would be the hero.

But in all the excitement over his heroics, Cramer didn't down the ball. Instead he tried to run it out of the end zone. In less time than it takes to say, "That was a dumb thing to do," Cramer was hit by end Steve Gauntry and fumbled the ball on the one-yard line, where Waddy recovered it for Colorado.

Two plays later, Buffalo fullback Jim Kelleher bulled in for the winning touchdown and a 13–10 lead with just forty-three seconds left in the game. Colorado sealed the Cowboys' fate by picking off a last-ditch pass and returning it twenty-five yards for another touchdown in a stunning 20–10 victory.

As if it wasn't bad enough to lose a game, Cramer's screw-up cost his team an invitation to a major bowl. At the end of the 1976 season, the Cowboys tied for the conference championship with Oklahoma and Colorado. But because Colorado beat Oklahoma and Oklahoma State, the Buffaloes received the coveted invitation to the Orange Bowl.

If only Cramer had downed the ball when he intercepted it, Oklahoma State would have won the title outright. And it would have gone to the Orange Bowl instead of to the relatively minor Tangerine Bowl.

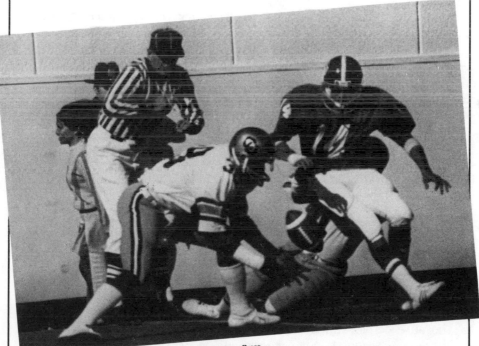

Cramer going from hero to zero   *Stillwater NewsPress*

Don't Play It Again, SMU

The Southern Methodist University Mustangs were penalized for unsportsmanlike conduct even though the players did nothing wrong. However, their band did.

During a game against the Texas A & M Aggies on November 1, 1986, the SMU band was warned at halftime to tone down their music when the Aggies were calling signals. But the musicians played on. With eighteen seconds left in the game and A & M winning 39–35, officials finally flagged the band for playing too loudly while the Aggies were trying to call signals.

The fifteen-yard penalty handed A & M an important first down and allowed the team to run out the clock.

Chris Ault

Coach ■ University of Nevada–Reno Wolf Pack ■ September 17, 1983

Head coach Chris Ault literally ran out on his team.

With 8:34 remaining in the game between his University of Nevada–Reno Wolf Pack and the Fresno State Bulldogs, Ault's running back, Otto Kelly, scampered eighty-nine yards for a touchdown and a 22–21 lead.

During the run, the coach got so caught up in the excitement that he began racing down the sideline alongside Kelly. When Ault reached the Fresno State twenty, he realized he had gone beyond the marked-off area of the bench and risked being penalized fifteen yards. So Ault just kept right on running! He dashed through the end zone, up a ramp, and out of Fresno State's Bulldog Stadium.

Ault was found hiding behind a truck by a fan who asked, "Say, aren't you the coach for Reno?" Without a moment's hesitation, Ault replied, "I'm just looking for a hot dog stand."

When the chagrined coach made it back to the bench, he learned his team had been penalized fifteen yards on the subsequent kickoff because he had run afoul of the rules. This gave good field position to Fresno State, which went on to kick a last-second field goal for a 24–22 victory over the Wolf Pack and Ault—who simply ran out of luck.

Wichita State Shockers

September 20, 1986

With a colossal 35–3 lead early in the third quarter, it seemed impossible for the Wichita State Shockers to lose its game against the Morehead State Eagles. But then Wichita State played with never-say-win abandon.

When the final gun sounded, the Shockers had suffered the most atrocious fall-from-ahead loss in NCAA history. They stumbled and tumbled to a 36–35 record-setting loss, the biggest lead ever blown in college football—thirty-two points.

"I've been coaching for thirty years and I have never, ever, ever lost a ball game like this," lamented WSU coach Ron Chismar. "It's a disgrace."

The sorry losers proved they couldn't hold on to a lead if it was handcuffed to them. In the second half, Wichita State committed two turnovers, missed a field goal, and made several crucial infractions on defense. The Shockers fumbled on their first possession of the third quarter and the Eagles quickly capitalized on the turnover by making a touchdown and a two-point conversion. Following a forty-seven-yard MSU field goal later in the period, Wichita State got off a sick eight-yard punt that went out of bounds on its own twenty-nine-yard line. Two plays later, Morehead State scored another TD and a PAT to cut the once-wide margin to 35–21.

The Shockers continued to rest on their butts—which was exactly where the Eagles were kicking them. Nevertheless, Wichita State still enjoyed a fourteen-point lead with less than three minutes to go in the game. Morehead State had the ball on its own twenty-yard line, so there seemed little cause for concern. After all, how could the Shockers possibly give up fifteen points in such a short span of time?

Here's how: Wichita State's secondary apparently decided to quit work early, because it took Morehead State quarterback Adrian Breen only three passes to get into the end zone. Following the extra point kick, the Shockers' seemingly insurmountable thirty-two-point lead had dwindled to just seven points with 1:54 remaining.

Everyone at Wichita's Cessna Stadium knew that the Eagles would try an on-side kick. All the Shockers had to do was fall on the ball. Instead, they fell apart. Morehead State recovered a perfectly executed on-side kick on its own forty-five-yard line. WSU knew it was

Thrown for a Loss

Teams That Couldn't Hold on to a Lead with Super Glue

- Miami Hurricanes. Blew 31–0 third-quarter lead over Maryland Terrapins, November 10, 1984. Lost 42–40. Held collegiate collapse record until Wichita State disaster.

- New Orleans Saints. Suffered most shameful fall-from-ahead loss in NFL history, December 7, 1980. Marched to twenty-eight-point halftime lead (35–7) over San Francisco 49ers. Lost 38–35 in overtime.

- Philadelphia Eagles. Set record for worst fourth-quarter collapse in NFL, December 1, 1985. Held 23–0 lead over Minnesota Vikings with 8:30 remaining. Lost 28–23.

- Buffalo Bills. Suffered most humiliating tie in pro football history, November 27, 1960. Enjoyed thirty-one-point lead (38–7) over Denver Broncos with 4:39 remaining in third quarter. Wound up tied 38–38.

- Yale Bulldogs. Held 29–13 lead and ball deep in Harvard Crimson territory with 3:34 remaining. Ended in nightmare tie. Reported Crimson campus newspaper: "Harvard Beats Yale 29–29."

doomed—and played like it. The Eagles—aided by a crucial pass interference penalty—marched fifty-five yards and scored a touchdown on a four-yard pass with just twenty-seven seconds left to play, slicing the margin to 35–34.

Morehead State elected to go for the tie, but Charlie Stepp's kick was wide. The Shockers began celebrating, relieved that they had given up thirty-one unanswered points yet were still going to win. But wait. The refs flagged Wichita State for offsides, giving the Eagles another chance.

Quarterback Adrian Breen ran to the sideline and pleaded with coach Bill Baldridge to go for the victory by trying a two-point conversion. "Coach," Breen said, "we've worked too hard for a tie. We deserve to win. You've got to have faith in us." Besides, the Wichita State defense looked like it was waiting for something terrible to happen. The wait was short. Breen took the snap from center, sprinted around end on a bootleg, and danced into the end zone untouched for the winning points.

Explaining how his team blew a thirty-two-point lead, WSU wide receiver Broc Fewin said, "We simply gave it away. It was a team effort." For Wichita State, the record-shattering defeat was a real shocker. At least fans and players will never have to endure further shame. At the end of the season, the university's administration shut down the school's football program.

Mike Friedman

Coach ■ University of Southern Colorado ■ September 1983

As a courtesy, Rocky Mountain Athletic Conference rivals Mesa College and Southern Colorado exchanged game films before their upcoming 1983 showdown.

But Mesa coach Bob Cortese didn't need a thumbs down from Ebert and Siskel to know that the game film submitted by Southern Colorado head coach Mike Friedman was the most deplorable in college football.

The footage had been deliberately doctored!

The week before his team was slated to play Mesa, Friedman agreed to send Cortese film of Southern Colorado's previous game with Idaho. Friedman then decided to add his own personal touch by reshooting the footage with some added elements. As the coach later admitted, he placed a number of objects—including thread, pieces of carpeting, and strips of celluloid—in front of the camera.

When Cortese looked at the game film, he was shocked and outraged. "You couldn't see the formations and coverages," he said. "The string got in the way of a bootleg play and you couldn't see who they were throwing to." Friedman also had cleverly blocked out where the Southern Colorado running backs lined up.

With an all but useless game film, Cortese said he had no choice but to use an extremely conservative game plan against Southern Colorado. As it turned out, the two teams tied, 14–14.

After the game, Cortese sent a letter and a copy of the doctored game film to Southern Colorado athletic director Bob Mullen, who ordered an investigation. Less than a week later, Mullen announced that Friedman, who was in his tenth year as head coach, had been "reassigned" effective at the end of the football season.

"I didn't think I did anything illegal," Friedman told the local press. "I was just trying to harass him." But Friedman went too far, turning a typical game film into a shameful B-movie.

Seattle Seahawks

November 4, 1979

In a moment of profound insight, someone once said football was a game of inches. But this was ridiculous.

In the most impotent offensive performance in the annals of the NFL, the Seattle Seahawks lost an average of 7.2 inches on each play—and finished the game with an ignominious record of minus seven yards in net yardage.

In a game against the Los Angeles Rams in the Kingdome, the Seahawks played as if they were peacefully observing the Sabbath. Never has a team played so long and done so little as Seattle. The team completed only *two* of seventeen passes, had just seven rushes that gained yardage, and made only one first down.

The Seahawks were so ineffective on offense that they never maintained control of the ball for longer than one minute and fifty-eight seconds. In their twelve possessions, they held the ball for a paltry total of 14:28 compared to the Rams' 45:32. Asked if he ever considered switching quarterbacks, coach Jack Patera said, "We didn't have the ball long enough to establish whether our quarterback was playing well or not."

Then again, no one needed much time to see that quarterback Jim Zorn couldn't move the team. Seattle's only first down came twenty seconds into the third period, when Zorn completed an eleven-yard pass to Steve Largent. That put the ball on the Seahawks' forty-two-yard line, the closest they got to the Rams' goal line all day! Three plays later—including a sack of Zorn—Seattle was back on its own thirty-four-yard line and Herman Weaver was called on to kick one of his eleven punts in the game.

The only question throughout the contest (won by Los Angeles 28–0) was whether the Seahawks' offensive yardage would hit double figures. They had only six yards at the half, but that was soon erased by six Ram sacks totaling fifty-five yards. It would have been worse except Seattle had the football for only thirty-five plays while their weary defense was forced to line up for ninety-five plays. The Seahawks did manage to pick up twenty-three yards by rushing in the right direction, but that was offset by the thirty yards they lost attempting to pass.

Although history was being made, for the 62,048 Seattle fans it was about as entertaining as the fourteenth-century black plague. The Seahawks set a franchise record for elapsed time in clearing out the Kingdome parking lot. It was accomplished by sending a few thousand fans in motion toward the exits in the third quarter. The rest left after they became too hoarse to boo any more.

After the game, a forlorn Zorn admitted, "Heck, I felt like booing, too."

Offensive Offense

The Seattle Seahawks lost their offense for one game; the Brooklyn Dodgers lost theirs for parts of two seasons. In 1942 and 1943, the Dodgers set a record in futility by getting shut out in six consecutive games.

The scoreless skein began in a game where Brooklyn's only threat ended with a blocked field goal. The next game, the team completed only one of eight passes for a single yard. In the following four games, the artless Dodger offense rushed for a net loss of eleven yards.

Brooklyn finally scored a touchdown on a twenty-five-yard desperation heave against the Chicago Bears. The Dodgers won only two games over the next two years and then died—from a terminal case of offensive anemia.

Colorado Mines-Colorado College Rivalry

1889–present

No rivalry has been more explosive than the one between the Colorado Mines Orediggers and the Colorado College Tigers.

Years ago, Mines students took the annual game so seriously that whenever their team lost to Colorado College, they sneaked over to the enemy campus in Colorado Springs and dynamited the Tigers' goal posts. In 1916, after the Orediggers were blown out 54–0, their supporters waited until the next morning to blow up the Tigers' goal posts with four big blasts.

Heaven help a Colorado College student who dared venture onto the Mines campus in Golden. According to Colorado College historian Juan Reid, "If Mines students caught a Colorado College guy on campus during the week before the game, they would burn an 'M' on his forehead with nitric acid."

In the early years of the oldest small college rivalry west of the Mississippi, the teams were made up of hard-nosed brawlers who hired and fired coaches without consulting the faculty or alumni. Both squads accused each other of using ringers—and both were right. Colorado College players included burly firemen and tough-as-nails Cripple Creek miners. Meanwhile, Mines called on the services of former football stars such as power fullback Lloyd Nordenholt, who had already made All-Big Ten for Michigan. For a while the games featured more broken bones, contusions, and concussions than points.

Eventually both schools quit suiting up football players who visited the campuses only on game days. There were no more guards and tackles with aliases. Thus, the teams played football the way it was meant to be played—tough but fair.

However, because the rivalry remained so bitter, football turned into an audience participation sport and the spectators incurred even more injuries than the players. For instance, halftime of a game between the two schools in 1920 turned into a bloody riot after both student bodies simultaneously began snake dances on the field. Naturally, they plowed into each other, triggering a wild free-for-all that involved nearly every attending male student from both schools. The melee delayed the start of the second half until police had a chance to break up the fights and cart away the wounded.

For years afterward, it was tradition for fans from both sides to swarm across the field before, during, and after the game looking for trouble—and finding it. "There were a lot of broken noses and several fans were hospitalized after Mines won 21–6 in 1954," said Reid.

Through 1986, the rivalry has remained fairly evenly matched on the field. Mines has won thirty-nine and Colorado College thirty-five with five ties. Fans stopped blowing up goal posts years ago—but it took a little longer—till 1951 to be precise—before they gave up stealing them.

For the 1951 clash, the undisputed championship of the Rocky Mountain Conference was at stake. Mines students chartered special railroad cars to haul them and their dozens of kegs of beer to Colorado Springs for the game. Shouting imprecations at local observers when the train arrived, the juiced-up visitors marched in a staggering, ragged column until they reached the stadium. There, they cheered the Orediggers on to a 14–6 triumph, Mines' first championship in twelve years.

Then the real fun began. Drunken Mines fans stormed the Colorado College goal posts while outmanned Tiger backers tried in vain to fend them off. The posts came crashing down, were dismantled, and carried back to the train. They had stolen the goal posts for a specific reason—to humiliate a traitor.

Recalled Mines coach Fritz Brennecke, "When the train arrived back in Golden, a delegation of those students still able to navigate took a section of the shattered goal post—which included nearly the full twenty-foot length of one of the uprights and part of the crossbar—and hauled it into the *Denver Post* building. They went up the steps into the office of sports editor Jack Carberry and presented it to him. He had picked Colorado College to win."

What NFL team gave up the most points in one quarter?

The Detroit Lions. Twice the Lions showed how defenseless their defense was. On October 7, 1945, against the Green Bay Packers, Detroit gave up forty-one points in the second period. Five years later, on October 29, 1950, the Lions reprised their act by surrendering forty-one points in the third quarter against the Los Angeles Rams.

THE HORSE RACING
HALL OF SHAME

Basic Witness

Atlantic City Race Track ▪ August 26, 1974

If the racehorse Basic Witness could talk, he'd recount a tale—or more accurately, tail—of woe.

Basic Witness was a six-to-one favorite to win the Longport Handicap stake race at Atlantic City Race Track when he was led into the starting gate. Jockey Carlos Barrera sat poised in the saddle as the back stall door was closed behind him.

Moments later, the starting gate opened with a clang and all the horses broke cleanly—except Basic Witness. He didn't go anywhere. Barrera gave him a kick and a whack but all the horse would do was paw frantically at the dirt. Only then did the jockey discover why his mount wouldn't move—Basic Witness had his tail stuck in the rear of the gate!

"No one, not even the old-timers, had ever seen anything like it," recalled Sam Boulmetis, the track steward at the time. "At first, we thought the horse just refused to race. Then we thought there was a tailing problem. Some horses will rear up in the starting gate, so a helper will stand in back on top of the gate and hold the horse's tail up. This is called tailing and it usually keeps the horse from rearing up.

"We figured that someone was tailing Basic Witness and forgot to let go, but the film didn't show anyone behind the horse. After talking to the starter and the jockey, we determined that somehow he got his tail caught just as they were closing the back stall door of the starting gate."

Because of the mishap, Basic Witness was declared scratched and all money wagered on him was refunded.

"It was a hell of a funny sight," said Boulmetis. "Thank goodness he didn't break real hard or he would have lost his tail for sure."

What world-renowned jockey lost his first 250 races?

Eddie Arcaro. After mounting nothing but losers for months on end, Arcaro eventually went on to win 4,779 races.

Willie Shoemaker

Kentucky Derby ■ May 4, 1957

As one of the all-time great jockeys, Willie Shoemaker can stand tall in the saddle—unless, of course, it's during a race. Shoe pulled such a boner in the 1957 Kentucky Derby and lost the race.

The day before Willie was to ride Gallant Man, the colt's owner, Ralph Lowe, told the jockey, "I dreamed last night that my rider had misjudged the finish line in the Derby." Shoe just laughed at the nightmare and said, "Oh, don't worry about that, Mr. Lowe. That's never going to happen to me. I've been riding too long to allow something like that."

But the next afternoon it happened to Shoemaker. Charging up on the outside after the final turn, Willie made his move as Gallant Man shot from third into the lead heading down the stretch. When his mount galloped past the sixteenth pole, Shoe triumphantly stood up in his stirrups, thinking he had crossed the finish line a winner. He hadn't. All he had done was turn the colt's owner into a prophet. Realizing he had confused the sixteenth pole for the finish pole, Willie sat down again, but his blunder had slowed Gallant Man's even stride for a fraction of a second. That's all it took to lose the race by a nose to eight-to-one Iron Liege.

Recalling that shameful day, the jockey admitted in a published account, "There can be no excuse for such a terrible and costly moment. . . . At Churchill Downs, the finish line is about a sixteenth of a mile farther toward the first turn than at any other race track in this country. I'm used to normal finish lines, and in the heat of battling Iron Liege through the stretch, I thought the sixteenth pole was the finish—and I stood up. Right away, I realized I had made a mistake." He said he will always believe that his goof was the difference between winning and losing.

The Derby wasn't the only time Shoemaker blew a major race. It happened the year before when he was riding Swaps in the 1956 Californian at Hollywood Park. "Swaps hadn't run in about a month and a half," he said. "We wanted him to win, naturally, but didn't want to abuse him if he was winning easily. On this day, he looked like he was going to win easily. At the eighth pole, I looked around and saw I was about three or four lengths in front, so I kind of eased up and relaxed. I got Swaps to relax also . . . when [suddenly] I saw Porterhouse flying by us on the outside. I couldn't get Swaps to run again

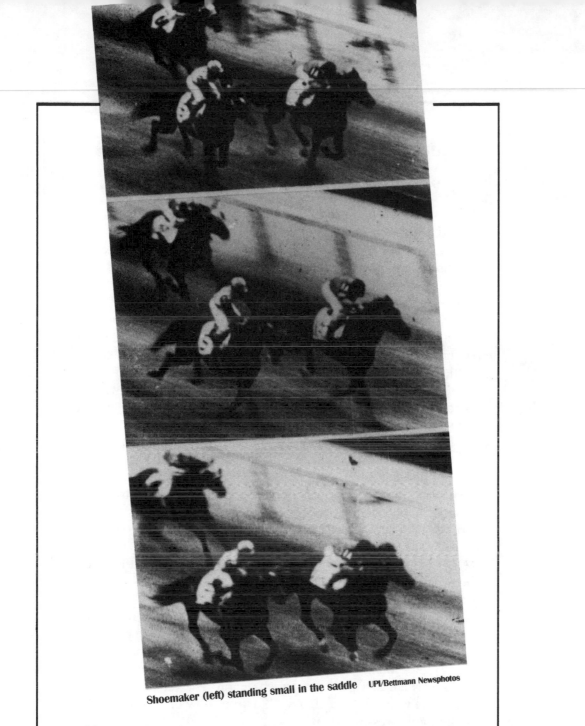

Shoemaker (left) standing small in the saddle   UPI/Bettmann Newsphotos

quickly enough, and we got beat by a head right at the finish. It was my fault."

But it is the Derby gaffe that Shoemaker will always be saddled with. Some good did come out of that embarrassing moment—it reined in a galloping ego. "At the time," he said, "I was beginning to believe that I was just the greatest, that I couldn't do anything wrong." At the '57 Derby, Willie Shoemaker discovered otherwise.

James Felton   Rudy Campas

Del Mar Race Track ▪ **September 12, 1973**

Jockeys James Felton and Rudy Campas galloped to shame when they duked it out with each other on horseback—during the race!

At the Del Mar Race Track in California, the two jockeys, who despised each other, rode long shots in the same race. Felton was on fifty-eight-to-one Only Way To Fly while Campas was aboard thirty-five-to-one Always Anxious.

When Campas carried Felton wide on the first turn, Felton cursed out his foe and then took off after him. As the jockeys turned into the stretch—their horses were eighth and ninth in a ten-horse field—the battle raged on.

Felton, on the rail, raised his whip and savagely lashed at Campas's head, striking him at least three times. As they crossed the finish line side-by-side and stride-for-stride, Campas retaliated. Angrily, he reached over, collared Felton by the neck, and yanked him from the saddle.

As Felton began to fall, he grabbed Campas's saddle to keep from tumbling to the turf. Unfortunately, one of his feet was caught in his own stirrup. Giving new meaning to the phrase "stretch drive," Felton found himself extended between the two charging mounts for several strides, his hands on one horse, his foot on the other. He looked more like a Hollywood stunt man than a jockey.

"Campas held Felton by the scruff of the neck while Felton was between the two horses, and then Campas just dropped him to the track like a sack of garbage," recalled race track spokesman Dan Smith. He witnessed the bizarre fight, which resulted in both jockeys being set down for ten days. "Felton wasn't hurt bad. He just had the wind knocked out of him. That was one really strange incident."

Trainer Johnny Longden, who as a jockey won more than 6,000 races, was the first person to reach Felton. The old-timer looked at the dazed young rider and said, "Kid, from now on, do your fighting in the jocks' dressing room."

What horse had the worst third-place finish in Kentucky Derby history?

Layson, in 1905. There were only three starters in the race! In his career, Layson ran in ninety-one races and won only three.

Sunshine Park/Florida Downs

Oldsmar, Florida ■ 1947–80

Sunshine Park wasn't one of the worst tracks in the country—it was *the* worst.

Horses sometimes had to leap over alligators at the turns and dodge deadly snakes on the backstretch. Fans had to sit on splintered benches and referred to the ramshackle Sunshine Park as "Shoeshine Park" because they needed shoeshines after walking through the mud of the parking lot.

It was an ugly, dirty, end-of-the-line track for jockey has-beens and never-weres; the final stop before the glue factory for slow-footed "thoroughdreads."

Today the track is called Tampa Bay Downs, having been saved and refurbished in 1980 by everyone's favorite horse trader, George Steinbrenner. But no amount of remodeling can cover up the track's shamefully checkered past.

"God, it was awful," declared Bob Cicero, track photographer since the original place opened up in 1947.

"The alligators were a big problem. In the early days, the big pond in the middle of the infield was filled with 'gators," he recalled. "You had to dodge around them and the fans had to look out for them in the parking lot. Sometimes there were as many 'gators watching the races as people."

As the horses made their way around the one-mile oval, they had to contend not only with alligators but rattlesnakes and cottonmouths as well. "The snakes slithered all over the place, especially after a heavy rain," said Cicero. "At least two horses were killed when they got bit by rattlers. It wasn't any great loss considering how bad the horses were."

The horses were so slow they could have been timed with an hourglass. "They raced here because they couldn't race anywhere else," said Cicero. "They were terrible. That's one of the reasons why you couldn't get a bookmaker in the country to take a bet on a race at Sunshine Park."

The other reason was that many of the races were blatantly fixed. "They couldn't make any money with the purses, which were nothing to begin with, so they did tricks with the races," said Cicero. "There was a famous old saying here: 'This horse will win if it takes half an hour.' In other words, when the fix is on, this horse will win no matter how slow he is."

The bad horses and big fixes weren't the only things that stunk up the joint. So did the water. "The place smelled like rotten eggs because the water had so much sulfur in it," said Cicero. "It was terrible. Every time people left the track, the smell stayed with them."

Not that there were that many horse players who went to Sunshine Park. The average handle was only $80,000, about ten times less than the typical handle at a respectable track such as Hialeah. Few bettors were desperate enough for action that they'd drive from the Tampa–St. Petersburg area on a two-lane country road where cows and pigs had to be shooed away, then tromp through thick mud in the parking lot, sit on rickety old benches in a smelly track under the broiling Florida sun, and lay money on snake-dodging nags. No wonder the track never turned a profit until 1977.

Sunshine Park, which was renamed Florida Downs in 1965, floundered under a succession of owners. "Once they got in here, they found out how bad the place really was and couldn't wait to get out," said Cicero.

Management could never get its act together. Take, for instance, the starting gate crisis. Said Graham Ross, public relations director of Tampa Bay Downs, "One time, right after the horses left the gate, the tractor broke down while it was pulling the starting gate off the track and onto the infield. If the gate didn't get moved in time, it would block the finish. So some of the fans leaped out of the stands, ran to the rail, and tried to warn the jockeys with handkerchiefs. But the jockeys had their heads down and never even looked up as they rounded the final turn. Finally, about twenty other people ran onto the track and helped the gate crew push the gate off just as the horses galloped by. The rest of the people in the stands were probably taking bets on whether the gate would make it off the track in time."

Typical of the track's bush image was the laughable discovery made shortly before Steinbrenner reopened the place under the Tampa Bay Downs banner. New measurements revealed that, for years, the furlong poles had been incorrectly placed. That meant that the times of all the thousands of races run at Sunshine Park and Florida Downs were dead wrong!

Nip and Tuck Race

The performance of one horse at the 1980 Tremont Stakes at New York's Belmont Park was a bit too shameful for fans. Galloping down the stretch, Great Prospector appeared so angry when Golden Derby caught up with him that Great Prospector bit Golden Derby in the face!

Apparently, Great Prospector bit off more than he could chew. Golden Derby still won the race.

Prix des Alpes

Steeplechase ▪ Cagnes-sur-Mer, France ▪ December 22, 1968

The Prix des Alpes was supposed to be a steeplechase race, but it turned into a four-legged demolition derby.

The event, run at Cagnes-sur-Mer, near Nice in southern France, was an unmitigated disaster from the start. The entire field of eleven horses performed as if they had been trying out for comedy roles in *Blazing Saddles.*

At the very first water jump, three mounts put on the brakes, catapulting their riders into the pond. Figuring they'd be in a lot of trouble for such horseplay, the steeds high-tailed it out of there.

Farther along the course, another jumper lost his rider after trying to go through a fence rather than over it. By the halfway point, three other horses imitated rodeo broncos and parted company with their riders.

Now only four jumpers remained in the race. The steed in the lead, Gingembre, managed to master most of the obstacle course and was only a couple of furlongs from the finish when she took a wrong turn and galloped off the course. This gave Oxtail and Poisson Rouge the perfect opportunity to vie for first. But apparently they had no horse sense for direction either, because they got lost, too, and ended up off the course and out of the running.

Now it was down to a one-horse race. The lone survivor, a filly named Fanita, simply had to make the last jump and trot home for the win. However, in keeping with the theme of this particular steeple-chase, she obstinately refused to jump the final hurdle. Instead, she threw her jockey, Jacques Fricotelle. He remounted, much to her annoyance, so she tossed him again. Then she took off. Fricotelle, refusing to give in to a temperamental filly, chased Fanita several yards down the course before he caught her and climbed back on.

Somehow he convinced Fanita to get over the jump. Then, just to make sure nothing else bad would happen, Fricotelle carefully walked her to the finish line of the most shameful steeplechase race ever run.

THE AUTO RACING
HALL OF SHAME

Buddy Baker's Wild Ride

Smokey Mountain Raceway ■ June 6, 1968

In all of auto racing, no ride was more ridiculous, more absurd, or more shameful than Buddy Baker's.

During a race at the Smokey Mountain Raceway near Maryville, Tennessee, the veteran driver's Dodge blew a tire, went out of control, and smashed into a cement wall on the first turn. Dazed and hurt, with a slight concussion and fractured ribs, Baker needed to get to the hospital.

"At that time, the vehicle we used as an ambulance was an old hearse," recalled Don Naman, then general manager of the track and now director of the Talladega Raceway. "The medics put Buddy on a stretcher with wheels and loaded him into the back of the hearse. But when they closed the back door, they forgot to latch it."

You don't need a great imagination to figure out what happened after the ambulance driver floored the gas pedal. The back door flung open, and out flew Buddy on a runaway gurney that began zipping down the track.

"There I was strapped to this stretcher and it was rolling clean across the track on the back straightaway in front of everybody," Baker recalled. What really terrified him was when he saw all the other race cars—riding around the track under the caution flag— heading straight toward him. "I told myself, 'Ain't this something. Here I survive a crash head-on into a cement wall and now I'm gonna get killed on a rolling stretcher.'"

Meanwhile, Naman, who was driving the pace car ahead of the field, was coming off the second turn when he spotted Baker and the speeding gurney. "When I saw Buddy rolling right toward us, I waved the other cars over as close to the wall as we could get," said Naman. "Then we all watched Buddy ride past us on that stretcher. When I looked the other way, I saw the ambulance drivers chasing after him. It was the funniest damn thing I've ever seen."

The medics finally caught up with Buddy and wheeled him back to the hearse. But he refused to get into the back again. "I got myself off that stretcher and squeezed into the front seat with them," said Baker. "I didn't want to get killed laying down on a stretcher.

"But, man, during the ride to the hospital I kinda wished I had been knocked out. It was wild! They were running wide open and I'll be damned if they didn't go through a red light and a car pulled out in front of us. I thought, 'Oh no, here we go again!'" The hearse swerved in the nick of time to miss the car but it skidded up on the sidewalk and plowed into a bunch of garbage cans. It made it to the hospital with a flat tire and hardly any brakes.

"I was so relieved to get to the hospital in one piece that I almost jumped out and ran in there myself," said Baker. "After I was treated and released, they offered to drive me back to the track in that damn hearse, but I told them, 'Never mind. I'll find another ride.'"

Baker, who popped his cork over crazy ride   AP/Wide World Photos

Jerry Grant

Indianapolis 500 ■ May 27, 1972

How much can a few gallons of gas cost? For race car driver Jerry Grant it was more than $70,000.

During a critical moment of the 1972 Indianapolis 500, he fueled his car with gas that didn't belong to him—and got caught. As a result, Grant was assessed the costliest penalty ever in Indy 500 competition.

To the surprise of racing observers, Grant was leading the race with only thirteen laps to go and seemed en route to a major upset. But then he appeared to signal to his pit crew that he was running out of gas. To make matters worse, his tire had picked up a piece of metal.

Forced to make a fifth and unscheduled pit stop, Grant roared off the track but overshot his own pit and screeched to a halt in front of his teammate Bobby Unser's fuel tank. Unser had long since dropped out of the race and had no further use for his fuel. So Grant took gas from Unser's fuel tank and then charged back onto the track to duel it out with eventual winner Mark Donohue, who had taken over the lead. Grant never caught up, but did finish second for what would have been a hefty $95,257.89 purse for him.

But a protest was filed by George Bignotti, crew chief for third-place finisher Al Unser. Track officials confirmed that Grant had used some of Bobby Unser's fuel, which is a violation of the race rules. Each car is allowed only a specific amount of fuel during the race and must use only its own supply.

As a result of this infraction, track officials dropped Grant from second to twelfth place in the standings—the biggest position loss in modern Speedway history. Thus, the racers who finished between third and twelfth all moved up a notch. Because of his penalized fall, Grant wound up with a payoff of only $23,852.85. The illegal fueling cost him a whopping $71,405.04—the difference between second place and twelfth.

David Pearson

Rebel 500 ■ Darlington Raceway ■ April 8, 1979

Sometimes stock cars roar around a curve squealing on two wheels. But David Pearson tried to run a race on two wheels.

The Silver Fox, who has won more than his share of races because of his skill and smarts, left his brains at a pit stop during the 1979 Rebel 500 at Darlington Raceway.

Midway in the race, Pearson, who was running fourth, pulled his Mercury into the pits. His crack pit crew decided to change all four tires on the stop, but Pearson didn't bother to look at his pitmen. He kept his eyes glued to the leader, and eventual winner, Darrell Waltrip, who had also come in for a pit stop.

The preoccupied Pearson wrongly assumed his crew was changing the tires only on the right side of his car. When they finished with that side, they loosened the two left wheels. Then, to their complete surprise, Pearson gunned the motor. Crewman Eddie Wood yelled, "Whoa!" but Pearson thought Wood was shouting, "Go!"

Pearson fuming in his two-wheeler *Charlotte News/Elmer Horton*

So Pearson drove off, running over the lug wrench that one of the crewmen was using. Of course, Pearson's car didn't go very far. About fifty yards down pit lane, both left wheels flew off his car as it came to a screeching halt. The runaway wheels merrily bounded down pit row as wide-eyed crewmen dodged out of their way. Crew chief Hoss Ellington, who barely escaped getting run over by one of the wheels, said later, "It scared me. It almost took my head off."

Meanwhile, back in his two-wheeler, Pearson pounded his steering wheel in anger and embarrassment. "I was so intent on beating Waltrip out of the pits, I forgot about the four-tire change," Pearson explained later. "I didn't even realize the crew was on the left side of the car. Of all the things that have ever happened to me, I can't think of anything worse."

Glen Wood, whom Pearson was driving for, was steaming mad over the blunder. "We all make mistakes," said Wood, "but his was a big one."

After everyone cooled down, someone suggested that Pearson should think about "re-tiring."

Bobby Allison   Cale Yarborough

Daytona 500 ■ February 18, 1979

Grand National stock car drivers Bobby Allison and Cale Yarborough gave auto racing a black eye—which is what they tried to do to each other at the end of the Daytona 500.

In the most deplorable finish ever in the famed race, the veteran drivers duked it out on the backstretch after Cale and Bobby's brother Donnie crashed on the final lap.

It was a socko ending to a wild and tense race. During the last ten laps, while the rest of the cars were a lap or more behind, Donnie's Olds was carrying Yarborough's Olds in its slipstream. When Cale dropped below Donnie in an effort to take the lead, they began a deadly duel. Finally, Donnie turned his car sharply to the left to prevent Yarborough from sling-shotting past him. The cars collided, spun out of control, and came to rest on the infield grass.

"Cale had made up his mind he would pass me low and I had my mind made up he was going to have to pass me high," said Donnie. "When he tried to pass me low, he went off the track. He spun and hit me."

Though lapped, Bobby Allison pulled up his car to find out what had happened to his brother and ended up in the brawl with Yarborough. "When Bobby came over to find out if we were all right," Donnie recalled, "Cale went over and punched Bobby through the screen [of Bobby's left window]. Then he came at me and started calling me names. They broke it up, but I'll tell you one thing, the fight would have been a good one."

Reported Yarborough, "It's the worst thing I've ever seen in racing. Bobby slowed down so he could block me off and save the race for his brother. I had Donnie beat. I know how to win a race. They double-teamed me.

"My left wheels were over in the dirt and Donnie knocked me farther on the dirt. I started spinning and Donnie started spinning. I pulled over and asked Bobby why he did it. He bowed up [in Southern talk that means Bobby arched his body as if to get out of his car] and I swung at him."

Bobby bolted out of his car just as Cale whipped off his own helmet to use as a shield. After dodging a kick to the shin, Bobby grabbed Cale's leg and tried to flip him backward. Just then Donnie, brandishing his helmet, joined the fray. To the chagrin of racing officials, the melee was witnessed by millions of fans on national TV.

The fuse that ignited the fight had been laid down earlier in the race when Donnie, Bobby, and Yarborough were running one, two, three when they all spun off the track after an accident. Donnie lost one lap, Bobby two, and Cale three. But Yarborough fought back into contention and, with ten laps to go, he was roaring along only inches behind the front-running Donnie.

The dramatic last-lap crash and fight were costly in more ways than one. The collision took Donnie and Cale out of the lead—and out of the race—allowing Richard Petty, who was running third, to zoom into first place and score a one-length victory over Darrell Waltrip. Petty, who won the first place prize of $73,900 that otherwise would have been copped by either of the original leaders, admitted that if it hadn't been for the backstretch crash, he would not have won. A.J. Foyt came in third, followed by Donnie Allison and Yarborough.

"I'm very disappointed because I lost my chance for a fourth Daytona 500 victory," said Cale. "I also lost the first place prize money, a $60,000 race car, and probably another $20,000 in endorsements."

What he hadn't included was the resultant $6,000 fine levied

Allison (left) and Yarborough in socko finish   AP/Wide World Photos

against him and each of the Allison brothers by the National Association for Stock Car Auto Racing. Donnie was also placed on six months' probation for running Yarborough off the track. However, NASCAR found no evidence that Bobby had tried to block out Cale.

"They got off easy," said Yarborough. "The fines came from what happened after the crash. No doubt about it, I was done in." Maybe so. But because of the driving trio's shocking actions, the world of auto racing was done in, too.

In Arrears

Driver Buddy Baker could have kicked himself in the butt for the rear-ender he caused at the Texas World Speedway.

Driving for Cotton Owens, Baker held a two-lap lead over the field when he looked at his pit board. It read, "You got it made." Baker would have had it made if only he hadn't spent so long gazing at the message. With his eyes on the board, Baker plowed right into the rear end of a car driven by James Hylton and wound up out of the race.

Myron Caves

Car Owner ■ Indianapolis 500 ■ May 17–25, 1969

Owner Myron Caves could have had his car in the Indianapolis 500's most coveted starting position—the pole. But thanks to his lame-brained strategy, he wrecked any chance of even making the field.

Back then, the rules stated that only those drivers who qualified during the first day of time trials were eligible for the pole. Each driver had three chances to qualify for the race by being one of the thirty-three fastest. On the first day of time trials for the 1969 Indy 500, it was wet and blustery, so the veteran drivers had a gentlemen's agreement that no one would attempt to qualify.

But late in the afternoon, Caves sent out his rookie driver, Jigger Sirois, to qualify. Jigger obediently hopped into his Quaker State Gerhardt-Offenhauser and headed around the slick, wet track. All he had to do was go four laps at a speed that would be better than the slowest qualifier and the pole position would be his.

He recorded speeds of 161.783, 162.279 and 160.542 m.p.h. in the first three of the required four laps. But, although they were solid times, Caves wasn't satisfied. He wanted faster speeds. So he waved Jigger in before the driver could complete his fourth lap.

The next day, Sirois went out again, recording speeds of 162.308, 162.660, and 162.376 m.p.h. Caves was just as unhappy as the previous performance and ordered Jigger back to the pits after finishing the third lap.

Caves didn't know what unhappiness was until the following day when Sirois's final attempt at qualifying failed because his engine broke a valve on the first lap.

What a shame. The slowest qualifier in the race was Peter Revson, who averaged 160.851. Had Caves let Jigger complete the fourth lap at a speed of at least 160 m.p.h. in either of his first two qualifying attempts, he would have qualified. Not only that, but Caves's car would have secured the pole position. Instead, Caves's car didn't even make it into the race. Poor Jigger never got another chance to drive in the Indy 500.

But his name won't be forgotten by the race world. The American Automobile Racing Writers and Broadcasters Association initiated a trophy called the Jigger Award. It's presented each May at the Indianapolis Motor Speedway to the driver deemed to have encountered the dumbest or most unlikely happening during the time trials of the Indy 500.

Kevin Cogan

Indianapolis 500 ■ May 30, 1982

Screamingly high speeds were no problem for driver Kevin Hogan. As the second-fastest qualifier for the 1982 Indianapolis 500, he had roared around the track at 204 m.p.h.

His problem was handling low speed. In the quickest and most shameful crackup in Indy 500 history, Cogan triggered a four-car crash before the race even started—on the 80 m.p.h. pace lap!

Cogan, then a second-year Indy driver who started in the front row, lost control of his car as the field approached the green flag. He veered right, clipping A.J. Foyt, and then careened into the path of Mario Andretti, setting off a chain reaction that knocked Cogan, Andretti, Roger Mears, and rookie Dale Whittington out of the race.

Fortunately, no one was injured. Whittington emerged from his ruined car, disgustedly holding up his useless and broken steering wheel. Cogan, meanwhile, walked over to the veteran Andretti who, after climbing out of his wreckage, shoved Cogan with both hands and shouted, "Get away from me, you hot dog!" When Cogan tried to explain what happened, Andretti showered him with curses and again pushed him away.

Cogan later told the press his car spun out of control because something broke or somebody hit him. But Andretti said, "He was in first gear and he tried to get the jump on everybody to the flag and he spun out. He did exactly what you're not supposed to do.... He crowded Foyt and he obviously wasn't paying attention to what he was doing. He couldn't handle the responsibility of the front row."

Asked what Cogan said to him, Andretti replied, "The usual alibis." And what did Andretti say to the kid? "You don't want to hear it."

Just as upset was Dale Whittington, who was making his Indy debut. The Cogan-caused crash left Whittington's car so damaged that it couldn't make the restart. Whittington never returned to the track and thus was given the dubious distinction of being the only qualifier never to have taken the green flag. He had Kevin Cogan to blame for that.

Whittington and his wheel of misfortune   UPI/Bettmann Newsphotos

Jack Ingram

North Carolina State Late Model Championship ■ September 14, 1986

Stock car driver Jack Ingram got his sporting events confused. He competed in an auto race, but drove as if he were in a demolition derby.

While battling for the lead in a race at New Asheville Speedway in North Carolina, Ingram's car tangled with two others and was knocked off the track. Ingram was so enraged that he turned his car around and, like an enemy destroyer hell-bent on sinking a stricken little PT boat, deliberately rammed one of his competitors.

Ingram, NASCAR's Busch Grand National points leader at the time of the race, had stayed ahead of the pack for the first 141 laps of the two-hundred-lap North Carolina State Late Model Championship race. But then Ronnie Pressley grabbed the lead on the 142nd lap. When Ingram tried to recapture first place, his car, along with Pressley's and Larry Ogle's, banged into each other. Ogle's car went to the outside and Pressley's slid into a wall just above the entrance to pit row while Ingram's car spun out.

Convinced that he had been wronged, Ingram didn't just get mad. He got even. He backed up, turned his car around on the infield grass, took dead aim on Pressley's disabled car and roared right into it. Pressley wound up in the hospital for treatment for crash injuries. Meanwhile, Ingram's shocking action sparked a wild brawl among several pit-row crewmen.

In the flurry of fisticuffs, police ordered Ingram to hop into his personal truck and leave the premises immediately. The next morning, he was served warrants charging him with three counts of assault on a law enforcement officer and one count of disorderly conduct.

The stock car veteran, who was seeking his sixth national racing title, received more bad news. Ed Cox, NASCAR administrative competition director, had witnessed the ramming and fined Ingram $5,000, suspended him for two races, and put him on probation for the remainder of the season.

At first Ingram claimed NASCAR's punishment was "kind of harsh because it was totally an accident." But then he later confessed, "My conduct in this incident was detrimental to the sport and I wish it hadn't happened." Racing fans everywhere shared the same wish.

Checkered Past

Four Inglorious Moments at the Indy 500

• 1912—Driver Ralph Mulford was told he would have to complete the full five hundred miles to earn tenth-place money. Since no one else was left in the race, he drove at a little-old-lady pace, stopping occasionally to get some fried chicken for himself and his riding mechanic. Mulford finally chugged home just before dark—eight hours, fifty-three minutes after the start of the race. The finishing rule was changed the next year.

• 1923—A design change in the Dusenberg race cars brought some extensive, last-minute work on the machines at a factory in downtown Indianapolis. The work was completed just a few hours before the race. Frantically, the drivers roared off toward the track, but they got caught in a massive traffic jam. By the time they arrived at the speedway, the race had already started without them and all they could do was watch.

• 1934—Driver Charlie Tramison failed to qualify because his car consumed its allotted supply of fuel before completing the trial run. This was particularly embarrassing to Tramison and his sponsor. The car was called "The Economy Gas Special."

• 1947—Near the end of the race, driver Bill Holland was cruising to what appeared to be a sure victory when his pit crew gave him the "EZY" sign. Wrongly believing that he had more than a full-lap lead over his nearest competitor, Holland wasn't concerned when his friend and fellow driver Mauri Rose pulled even with him. In fact, Holland charitably waved him by. Rose took the lead and the checkered flag. The chagrined Holland finished second.

Ricky Rudd

Atlanta 500 ■ March 23, 1975

Ricky Rudd turned into a hit-and-run driver in his first major race. There were no injuries—except to his pride.

"My first time on the big speedway was a little embarrassing to say the least," confessed Rudd as he recounted his shameful debut made during the Atlanta 500 at the Atlanta International Speedway.

Rudd, who was nineteen at the time, was driving a 1973 Ford Torino fastback when two cars tangled in front of him on the fourth turn. "I slammed on the brakes and spun out," Rudd recalled. "I skidded down the frontstretch backwards against the wall. It was my first time in an accident and I knew I had to get out of there real fast. The crash happened on the side of the fuel filler and I was sure the car was going to catch fire and blow up. So I unbuckled my seat belt and ran across the track and jumped over the pit wall to safety.

"A NASCAR official came over to me and said, 'What's the matter?'

"And I said, 'My car is all smashed up and it's ready to burst into flames.'

"'No it's not,' he said. 'All you did was scrape a little paint off your car. Now go out there and move it because it's blocking the track!'

"Shoot, all this time I thought I had destroyed it," said Rudd.

Darren Crowder

Winston 500 ■ May 4, 1986

The strangest, most bizarre race ever run on a track featured speeding, siren-shrieking police motorcycles and squad cars—and a front-running stolen pace car.

Crowder setting the wrong pace   AP/Wide World Photos

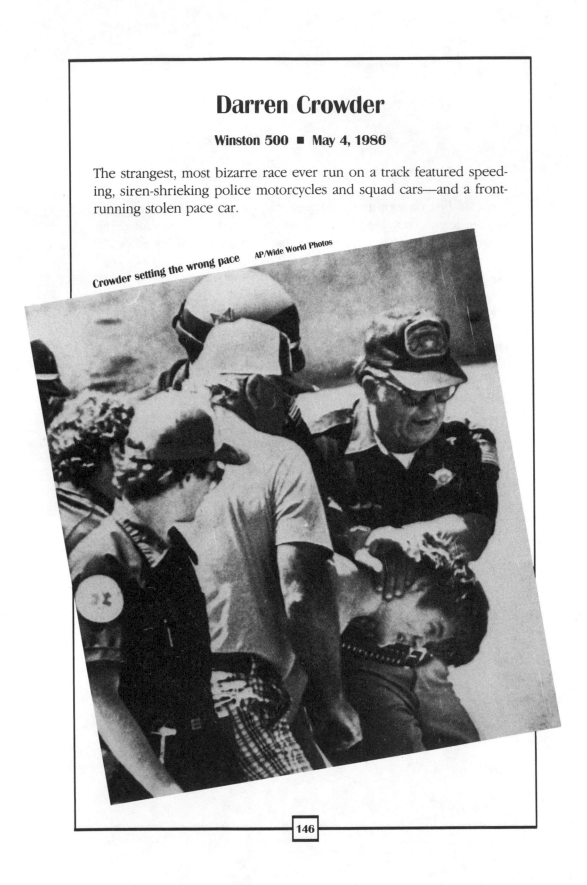

Shortly before the start of the Winston 500 NASCAR race at the Alabama International Motor Speedway in Talladega, fan Darren Crowder was admiring the shiny new Pontiac Trans-Am pace car sitting in front of the main grandstand. It was then he noticed that the keys to the unoccupied car were still in the ignition.

To Crowder, who had always wanted to ride in a pace car, the temptation was just too great to overcome. Before anyone could stop him, the twenty-year-old fan from Birmingham hopped into the car and roared off down the track.

"He was really lead-footing it around the track," recalled raceway director Don Naman. "Fortunately, the whole track was cleared at the time because the race was supposed to start in five minutes."

But first track officials had to contend with a different race. Police in motorcycles and squad cars zoomed onto the track in pursuit of the pace car, which squealed through the 2.66-mile circuit at speeds up to 100 m.p.h. Crowder would have held the lead for a second lap if it hadn't been for a blockade of track safety and maintenance trucks across the fourth turn.

Crowder screeched to a stop and conceded the race to police who quickly carted him off. "That guy was something of a hero around here for a while, although he sure did embarrass us," said Naman. "That incident taught me you can never be too careful. Hell, even a pace car ain't safe if you don't lock it up."

Lloyd Ruby

Indianapolis 500 ■ May 30, 1969

During a pit stop that he will always regret, 1969 Indianapolis 500 leader Lloyd Ruby became too impatient and took off. Unfortunately, what he took off was the side of his car. And that left him in the pits—in every sense of the word.

"I never felt worse in a race than I did during that one," said the veteran, considered one of auto racing's hard-luck drivers. Time and again, misfortune had beaten him to the Indy finish line. In 1966, he was black-flagged for an oil leak, and in 1968, he led for nineteen laps before a coil conked out. Two other times he lost the rear end of his car.

But in 1969 it looked like Ruby would outdistance the bad luck that had dogged him in past Indy 500s. He was driving a picture-perfect race in his Laycock-Offenhauser and was holding onto the lead on the 105th lap when he headed into pit row to refuel.

With military precision, his pit crew filled the car's two tanks, using a fueling hose that had a special locking device that attached to the gas-tank fitting on his car.

"I was sitting in the car, staring straight ahead, concentrating on the race, and getting ready to move out," Ruby recalled. "When the crewman had filled one of the tanks, I thought both tanks had been refueled so I moved out. Or at least I tried."

As Ruby jammed his foot on the accelerator and released the clutch, his car lurched forward only a few yards when he heard a sickening sound and felt an awful tug. By taking off for the track too soon, Ruby hadn't given his crew enough time to uncouple the fuel hose from his car's tank fitting. He had ripped out a vital section of the left side of his thin-skinned car—including the fuel tank. Gasoline spilled out onto the pavement in pit row, and with it went his chances of winning.

"When I got out of the car and looked at it, I just couldn't believe it," Ruby recalled. "In fact, I had to go back and look at it again and again. What a sickening sight. Everything had been running so smoothly and suddenly I was out of the race. I can't remember more disappointment than that day. It just seemed that the race wasn't meant for me.

"Three times I have felt like I was going to win the Indianapolis 500. Three times I have wound up with an empty feeling in my stomach. If that feeling comes from a broken heart, mine must be in a million pieces.

"I'd been racing for a long time and this was the first and only time that my refueling got so screwed up. It was just one of those freak things. I can laugh about it now, but, boy, it sure hurt back then."

THE OLYMPIC
HALL OF SHAME

Olympic Games

Paris ■ 1900

The Olympics have withstood boycotts, terrorism, fraud—and the Games of 1900.

The Games were so disorganized that many of the 1,330 competitors representing twenty-two countries didn't even realize they were participating in the Olympics.

The event was treated as a sideshow for the 1900 International Exposition in Paris. To make certain the Olympics wouldn't upstage the massive industrial exhibits of the exposition, the French government refused to use the word "Olympics" in the program of events. The Games were simply called "international championships."

The facilities were simply called awful. The track and field events were held on the grounds of the Racing Club of France, in the Bois de Boulogne, the main park in Paris. It was a terrific site—for picnicking, not running. The French refused to install a cinder track because they didn't want to disturb the grass. Runners had to race on a grass field that was uneven and in many areas was sloped. The hurdles—some were nothing more than broken telephone poles—had been hastily constructed over bumpy, bush-covered ground.

Discus and hammer throwers didn't even have enough room to compete. They watched, disconcerted, as their throws invariably landed in trees that surrounded the field. The discus champion hurled the discus into the crowd three times. French officials, lukewarm at best about the Games, never even considered removing the trees.

The jumpers were ready to jump out of their skins in frustration because they had no proper pits and were forced to dig their own pits with their cleated shoes. The vaulters had to use a wooden platform rather than thrust their poles into dirt.

Numerous internal problems within the French Olympic organizing committee left many of the sports without experienced officials, creating heartache and anger for several U.S. athletes. Two American pole vaulters, Charley Dvorak of Michigan and Bascom Johnson of New York, were told by French officials that the pole vault final would be held the following day. But just minutes after the two athletes went off by themselves to explore Paris, the officials changed their minds and staged the finals that afternoon—without Dvorak and Johnson.

The fifty-five American athletes were stunned by not only the poor planning but also the low attendance. At one time, there were more Olympians on the field than there were spectators in the stands. Most of the fans were American tourists. Despite the horrendous conditions, the Americans persevered and won seventeen of the twenty-three events.

They would have won eighteen, but they were cheated out of first place in the marathon. Originally, it was to be run on a course from Paris to Versailles. But at the last moment—after most of the runners had carefully studied the route—the French officials switched to a different course that included running through a maze of Parisian streets. Throughout the race, inept officials failed to check the runners properly and keep them from going astray. Several runners went off course, accidentally or otherwise.

The American favorite, Arthur Newton, took the lead at the midway point and was never passed on the road. He fully expected to be hailed as the winner when he trotted to the finish line. To his shock, he was told by officials that he had finished fifth—behind a Swede and three Frenchmen, including the alleged winner, Michel Teato, a Parisian bakery boy. There was little doubt that the Frenchman knew the course—and its detours—exceedingly well. Perhaps too well. Teato didn't look like he had run farther than a few blocks. "There wasn't a drop of mud on him or the other two Frenchmen," fumed American runner Walter Tewksbury. "Everyone else in the race was drenched with the stuff."

Teato's performance was hardly Olympian in character, but then neither were some of the events themselves. Among the "sports" included in the 1900 Games were croquet, fishing, billiards, and—believe it or not—checkers!

Marathon Race

St. Louis Games ■ 1904

No Olympic marathon race was more shameful than the one run in the 1904 Games in St. Louis.

The first runner who crossed the finish line was disqualified for hitching a ride in a car! The next runner did win the race, but only because he had been on drugs. The competitor who should have won ate too many green apples along the way and was slowed by cramps. Meanwhile, another contender lost a chance for the gold because he ran a mile off course trying to flee from an angry dog.

It was a race that was doomed from the start. The organizers of the event must have been graduates from Marquis de Sade University. They plotted a tortuous course of seven hills run on dusty roads in the middle of a hot, muggy ninety-degree afternoon.

Only fourteen of the thirty-two starters made it to the finish line. Many choked on the dust raised by dozens of autos carrying journalists, doctors, judges, and coaches that chugged alongside the runners.

More than three hours—about an hour longer than usual for a winner to finish a marathon—had passed before the first runner entered the stadium and crossed the finish line. Fred Lorz, of New York, was hailed as the winner. Looking remarkably fresh, he was photographed with Alice Roosevelt, the daughter of President Teddy Roosevelt, and was waiting to receive the gold medal. But then somebody called an indignant halt to the proceedings with the charge that Lorz was an imposter and the real winner was still somewhere in the distance. Officials then discovered that Lorz had actually ridden in a car for nearly half the race—so they disqualified him on the spot.

Lorz admitted that he quit running about nine miles out when he was seized with cramps. So he hopped into a car and rode for the next eleven miles along the race route, waving and joking with the other runners. But when the auto broke down about five miles from the finish line, Lorz, now fully recovered, jumped out and ran the rest of the way. When he entered the stadium, thousands of spectators rose to their feet and cheered him as the winner while he circled the track and crossed the finish line.

Lorz claimed it was just a prank and that he had no intention of continuing the joke, but he couldn't resist the cheers of the crowd. The unamused Amateur Athletic Union banned him for life from marathon competition. (However, the ban was lifted months later and Lorz went on to win the Boston Marathon the next year—without the help of a car.)

Lorz's practical joke took some of the edge off the reception the spectators gave to Tom Hicks, the real winner, when he arrived at the finish line. It was similar to a scene that happened sixty-four years later in 1968, when a hoaxer named Norbert Sudhaus stole the limelight from marathon winner Frank Shorter. Sudhaus had appeared on the track a couple of minutes before Shorter and ran a full lap before being hustled away by security guards.

Hicks's 1904 marathon victory was clouded by what may have been the first doping incident of the modern Games. With seven miles remaining in the race, Hicks was exhausted and ready to quit. But his handlers, who trailed him in an auto, refused to let him give up. They ran up to him and fed him the whites of egg laced with small doses of strychnine. The drug—later banned by Olympic rules—dulled Hicks's pain enough for him to keep plodding on. Throughout the rest of the race, his handlers gave him brandy and more strychnine.

Hicks staggered across the finish line in a daze—just as the furor over the Lorz hoax was subsiding—and had to be carried to a dressing room where four doctors worked to revive him. After the English-born brass worker from Cambridge, Massachusetts, accepted the gold medal, he promptly announced his retirement.

The runner who should have won the marathon was Felix Carvajal, a 5-foot-tall Cuban mailman. Unfortunately, he lost because he listened to his stomach instead of his brain.

Carvajal financed his trip to St. Louis through contributions of his countrymen. He traveled from Havana to New Orleans, where he was promptly relieved of his money in a dice game. Undaunted, he hitchhiked to St. Louis while subsisting on handouts. He was half-starved and exhausted when he arrived at the Games, where he was immediately adopted by a group of American athletes.

When Carvajal appeared at the starting line dressed in a long-sleeved shirt, long pants, and heavy boots, his new American friends delayed the race long enough for them to cut off his trousers at the knees and snip off his shirt sleeves. They also lent him a pair of low-cut shoes for the marathon.

With no formal training or knowledge of pace or timing, Carvajal ran an unorthodox race. He jogged tirelessly along the course, pausing here and there to talk with bystanders along the way. He laughed and cracked jokes in his broken English as if he were back on his job delivering mail.

While stronger and more experienced runners were dropping to the ground because of the heat and dust, the fun-loving little Cuban kept pace with the leaders—until his stomach got the better of him. He was so hungry that food became more important than the race itself. First, he snatched a couple of peaches from an official who was driving by. Then Carvajal detoured off the course into an orchard where he ate several green apples. Not surprisingly, he developed stomach cramps that forced him to take a lengthy rest. Even so, he managed to come in fourth. If he had just laid off the apples, Carvajal might have won the marathon.

Another runner who could have won was a South African Zulu tribesman named Lentauw. He ran well, finishing in ninth place. He would have done much better had he not been chased nearly a mile off course by a large and angry dog.

Anthropology Days

St. Louis Games ■ 1904

It was as if P.T. Barnum had been put in charge of the 1904 Olympics. Curious about the alleged agility, strength, and athletic feats of "savage and uncivilized tribes," the St. Louis Olympic Organizing Committee invited aboriginal peoples to compete in a two-day exhibition.

The event—called Anthropology Days—turned into a sham. The competitors were no athletes but aging, out-of-shape sideshow performers who engaged in ridiculous contests such as mud fighting, spear throwing, and pole climbing.

It would have warmed the heart of any showman—but it chilled the soul of all Olympians.

Olympic officials invited African Pygmies, South American Patagonians, Philippine Igorots, Japanese Ainus, Mexican Cocopas, and Sioux Indians. But rather than pick trained athletes from the tribes, officials chose natives who were in St. Louis appearing in sideshows at the city's special exposition. The tribesmen, some as old as fifty-seven, were in no physical condition to compete and weren't even familiar with most of the sports. They belonged on the athletic field about as much as corporate executives belonged in the Amazon jungle.

Nevertheless, the Olympic committee staged Anthropology Days—with predictably disastrous results. Spectators were aghast at the poor performances of the "savages." A newspaper account of the event complained that "the representatives of the savage and uncivilized tribes proved themselves inferior athletes. . . . An American Sioux Indian won the 100-yard dash in remarkably slow time [11.8 seconds], and an African Pygmy in the same event made a mark [14.6 seconds] that can be beaten by any 12-year-old. . . . The Patagonian could throw the shot only 10½ feet." An Ainu competitor recorded for the worst effort in the event with a pitiful toss of just thirty-nine inches. In the high jump, a giant Patagonian was able to leap all of three feet.

On the second Anthropology Day, the aborigines were permitted to perform any feats of strength, speed, or skill native to their own countries. But even then, these nonathletes failed to impress anyone. However, there were two high points of the show. A Philippine Igorot climbed unassisted up a vertical fifty-foot-high pole in twenty seconds and, according to an official account, "during the mud fight between the Pygmies, the tiny Africans showed remarkable ability to dodge and throw."

Calling Anthropology Days an "outrageous charade," Baron Pierre de Coubertin, the father of the modern Olympic Games, sighed and said, "In no place but America would one have dared to place such events on an Olympic program."

Roger Brousse

Boxing ■ Paris Games ■ 1924

Long before there was a shark named Jaws, there was an Olympic boxer who could have qualified for that moniker.

Frenchman Roger Brousse, a twenty-three-year-old middleweight, used not only his fists and footwork but his teeth to fight! Whenever he got into a clinch, he'd deliberately take a bite out of his opponent.

"It was found necessary to substitute for a mere boxer a man-eating expert named Brousse, whose passion for raw meat led him to attempt to bite off portions of his opponents' anatomies," reported the *London Daily Sketch*.

Boxing in front of his countrymen at the Velodrome d'Hiver in Paris during the 1924 Olympics, Brousse tried to make a meal out of Argentine fighter Eduardo Gallardo. The chomp champ gnawed on his foe every chance he got and punched and munched his way to victory. Gallardo put up a beef but officials refused to swallow the notion that any boxer would literally try to devour an opponent.

"Having got his teeth into a piece of Argentine meat," wrote another boxing reporter, "Brousse decided to vary the menu by sampling some of the unroasted human beef of Old England" in the person of Harry Mallin, the defending gold medal winner from Great Britain.

During a quarterfinal match against Mallin, Brousse once again tried to turn the boxing ring into a lunch counter. Throughout the bout, which he was clearly losing, Brousse dined on Mallin's chest.

For dessert, Brousse was named the winner by judges who were totally intimidated by the boisterous French crowd.

After the match, Mallin, who had never lost a fight, tore off his uniform top to show several sets of teeth marks on his chest. Although the referee refused to do anything about it, the International Boxing Association disqualified Brousse the next day—allowing a cannibal to compete in the Olympics was much too distasteful.

Antonius Lemberkovits

Shooting ■ Los Angeles Games ■ August 13, 1932

Hungarian marksman Antonius Lemberkovits was gunning for an Olympic gold medal. He would have won it, too, if only he hadn't hit the bull's-eye—on the wrong target.

The competition in the miniature carbine match at the 1932 Los Angeles Games was fierce. The world's best shooters were hitting tens (bull's-eyes) on the three-quarter-inch targets at fifty meters. Lemberkovits, who also was shooting flawlessly, had his sights set on a perfect three hundred score.

The Hungarian's aim was straight and true, his concentration unwavering and intense. Unfortunately, it was too intense. Midway in the match, he was so determined to hit another ten and keep his perfect streak alive that he forgot to look for his target number. He fired a bull's-eye on the target of the shooter next to him, Gustavo Huet of Mexico.

Lemberkovits immediately recognized his mistake and notified the range officials. They confirmed that he had fired at the wrong target. Even though he had hit a ten, the shot was scored a complete miss according to the rules.

What strange way was 1932 Olympic heavyweight boxing champion Santiago Lovell greeted when he returned to his homeland of Argentina?

He was arrested. While sailing home after the 1932 Games in Los Angeles, the Argentine athletes continually fought each other until the fed-up captain put them all in confinement under guard. When the ship docked at Buenos Aires, police were waiting to arrest the chief brawler—who was none other than Santiago Lovell.

Lemberkovits's dream of winning the Olympic championship had been shot down. Because of the miss and another shot just off the mark, he scored a 285. Had he hit his own target, he would have finished with a 295—enough to have won the gold medal.

Brazilian Olympic Team

Los Angeles Games ■ 1932

No Olympic team ever made a more pitiful arrival or departure than Brazil's.

Only a third of the team managed to show up; the rest were stranded on a ship because they were too broke to pay a head tax on foreign visitors. The whole team—and the Games—would have been better off if all the members had stayed on board. Although the Brazilians didn't come close to placing in any event, their water polo players made their presence felt. They triggered a melee that forced Olympic officials to kick them out of the Games.

When Los Angeles hosted the 1932 Summer Games, Brazil was one of the many nations that were financially crippled by the world-wide depression and couldn't find money to send a team to the Olympics. The country was in economic turmoil because the whole-sale price of coffee—its one and only cash crop—had fallen from twenty-five cents per pound to just seven cents.

But the Brazilian government figured out a way to send its team of sixty-nine athletes. It loaded them on a freighter along with twenty-five tons of coffee and told the athletes to sell the coffee at ports along the way to Los Angeles to finance their trip to the Olympics. So they set sail with high hopes—hopes that were all but sunk because hardly any port they visited wanted so much as a single coffee bean.

By the time the ship reached Los Angeles a week before the Game's opening ceremonies, the Brazilians had only $24 among them. They needed more money because the U.S. Immigration Service had levied a $1 head tax on every alien who visited America. The Brazilian consul in San Francisco tried to help out the broke team by dispatching a courier with a $45 check so all sixty-nine athletes could go ashore and compete. But before the courier arrived, the Brazilian currency had been devalued and the check—which had been drawn on a Brazilian bank account—was now worth only $17. But it didn't matter—no one would cash it anyway.

Undeterred, the Brazilian coaches chose the twenty-four athletes they thought would have the best chances of winning, paid their head tax, and sent them off to the Olympic Village. The team members who were left behind put out to sea again and sailed up to the Pacific Northwest in a last-ditch effort to sell their coffee. The ship wasn't seen again in Los Angeles until after the closing ceremonies.

Meanwhile, back at the Olympics, the Brazilians competed in track and field, swimming, water polo, rowing, and shooting. They won no medals and their best performance was a sixth-place finish in the pole vault.

Yet they were the talk—the bad talk—of the Games. In a rough first-round water polo match against Germany, the Brazilians kept fouling their opponents and vehemently protested the calls of referee Bela Komjadi of Hungary. Because none of the Brazilians spoke Hungarian, and Komjadi spoke no Portuguese, the team tried other means to make their feelings known.

At the end of the match, won by Germany 7–3, the Brazilians politely joined hands and gave a cheer for the winning team. Then they impolitely assailed Komjadi with vile oaths in their native tongue.

Weighty Dilemma

A South African lightweight boxer named Hamilton-Brown ate himself right out of a chance for a medal.

In the 1936 Games in Berlin, he lost an opening round match on a split decision. However, hours later, officials announced that one of the judges had mistakenly reversed his scores and that Hamilton-Brown had actually won the bout and was scheduled to fight again the next day.

By the time the boxer's manager found him and gave him the good news, it was after midnight—and too late. Hamilton-Brown had eased the pain of his defeat by going on an eating binge which caused him to gain five pounds.

This act of gluttony pushed the South African over the weight limit. His trainer desperately tried to boil him down, but it was no use. The next day, Hamilton-Brown failed to make the weight limit and was disqualified.

As the fuming-mad players headed for the referee's stand, Komjadi fled into the dugout surrounding the pool and shouted, "Police! Police!" Still shouting epithets, the Brazilians leaped down into the dugout where the terrified ref cringed in fear. Police rushed in and broke up the fracas before the players could get their hands on the squat, straw-hatted official.

After his rescue, Komjadi lambasted Brazil's allegations that he had favored the Germans. "The Brazilians have no idea how to play water polo," he declared. "They have no idea of the international regulations. It stands to reason that if I were to be unfair, I, as a Hungarian, would be prejudiced against the Germans, our big rivals, and not against Brazilians, whom we do not have to fear. I guess," he added with tongue in cheek, "I don't know the Brazilian rules."

The Olympic authorities were so outraged by the Brazilians' attack that the water polo team was banned from any further competition in the sport.

At the end of the Games, Brazil's Olympic squad was hustled back to their freighter where they rejoined their stranded comrades and sailed home—to further trouble. They arrived in Rio de Janeiro right in the midst of a full-blown revolution.

Robert Charpentier

Cycling ■ Berlin Games ■ August, 1936

Olympic cyclist Robert Charpentier was struck with such a bad case of gold fever that he was blind to good sportsmanship. Through a nasty bit of chicanery, he stole the gold medal from the cyclist who deserved to win it—his own teammate and good friend.

Charpentier and his fellow countryman Guy Lapebie were given the best chance of bringing a gold medal home to France in the 100-kilometer road race in the 1936 Berlin Games. But the Frenchmen had to contend with a narrow road crowded with more than one hundred cyclists. Through skill and experience, Charpentier and Lapebie avoided the numerous spills that marred the race. With Lapebie setting the pace, Charpentier was content to stay a fraction of a second behind as he plotted his strategy for a big finish that would win him the coveted medal.

As they neared the finish line, the two Frenchmen and eight other cyclists made an all-out sprint for the gold. Charpentier pumped his legs like pistons, desperately trying to catch up to his teammate, who held a lead of less than a bicycle length over him. With every ounce of strength he had, Charpentier inched closer and closer to Lapebie, as did the other eight frontrunners. But by now, it looked like there was no way Charpentier could win. Still, he was determined to capture the gold medal.

Suddenly and inexplicably, Lapebie slowed down only a few meters from the finish line. It was just enough for Charpentier to sprint past him and win the gold by a mere two-tenths of a second.

No one could explain why Lapebie had slowed down. Even he couldn't explain it. Spectators couldn't see what happened to him because he was in the middle of the closely bunched pack of ten cyclists who were separated from first place to tenth by just 1.6 seconds.

Only later, long after Charpentier had taken home his medal, was the mystery solved. A photograph shot a few meters in front of the finish line showed exactly why Charpentier won the race—he had grabbed Lapebie by the shirt tail and pulled him back!

Italian Soccer Team

Berlin Games ■ August, 1936

In one of the most deplorable examples of Olympic sportsmanship ever seen, the Americans played soccer while their Italian counterparts played sock 'em.

Battling as if World War II had already started, the Italians kicked, slugged, shoved, and tripped the Americans throughout a bloody first-round match in the 1936 Games in Berlin. Like merciless soldiers who never heard of the Geneva Convention, the Italians rode roughshod over the rules of the game—and over the beleaguered referee who tried futilely to halt their vicious tactics.

The Americans were not trained in warfare, yet they bravely managed to hold off their attackers until the casualties began to mount. Early in the second half, American star George Nemchik was brutally kicked in the stomach and forced to leave the game. A few minutes later, after the Italians had scored the lone goal of the game, American Bill Fiedler suffered torn ligaments in his knee when he was blatantly knocked out of bounds by Italy's Achille Piccini.

Referee Hans Weingaertner had seen enough and ordered Piccini from the game. But Piccini simply ignored him. Three times the ref tried to get the Italian off the field, but to no avail. Weingaertner finally gave up after the Italian players declared to all who cared to listen that the German ref was so incompetent as to be beneath any consideration. Just to underscore their contempt for him, six snarling, swearing Italian players swarmed around the ref, pinned his arms to his sides, and clapped their hands over his mouth.

Weingaertner meekly allowed the game—and the bloodshed—to continue. And with Piccini still in the lineup. After this scandalous show, the Americans protested, but the final score stood at 1–0.

Love Garden

Berlin Games ■ 1936

Only Hitler and the Nazis could twist the Olympic ideal into a scheme so wildly perverted it was the single most ridiculous sidelight to the 1936 Games.

Obsessed with creating an Aryan nation, the Nazis used the Berlin Olympics to lure unsuspecting athletes to a human stud farm where they were seduced by winsome young maidens who tried to have their babies.

To the Nazis, Olympic athletes were considered nearly perfect humans who would make ideal mating partners with the best of German womanhood. Unbeknownst to most of the outside world, the Nazis quietly set up an enthralling "Love Garden" behind the Olympic Village. It was there, in the midst of an idyllic beech forest, that the athletes were enticed by alluring damsels handpicked by the Nazis.

These tantalizing maidens were usually sports teachers or members of Hitler's youth groups and had passes to enter the Olympic Village so they could "mingle" with the athletes. They picked up only those young men who, because of their good looks and hard bodies, made ideal breeding prospects. Chosen for seduction were Aryan types—white Americans, Scandinavians, Dutchmen and, of course, Germans. These naive athletes were easily led into the "Love Garden." Among enchanting flowers, protective shade trees, and a pristine lake, nature just took its course.

Before submitting to the athlete of her choice, each temptress made sure her sexual partner gave her his Olympic badge. If she got pregnant, she gave his badge to a government maternity hospital to prove the Olympic origin of her infant. The state would then pick up the tab for the prenatal and postnatal care.

No one knows for sure how many Olympic babies were born or how many Olympians succumbed to Hitler's crazy mating scheme. However, there seemed to be an awful lot of happy losers. Perhaps that's because even though they didn't score on the athletic field, they sure did in the "Love Garden."

What future heavyweight boxing champion of the world was disqualified in the Olympics for not throwing a single punch in a gold medal bout?

Ingemar Johansson. During the 1952 Games in Helsinki, the Swede faced American H. Edward Sanders in the final match. Johansson spent all his time in the ring back-pedaling without taking a swing. The Swede was finally disqualified in the second round for "not giving of his best." Seven years later, Johansson landed enough punches to become the world heavyweight champ.

Vyacheslav Ivanov

Single Sculls ■ Melbourne Games ■ November 26, 1956

Of all the athletes who ever won an Olympic gold medal, none screwed up the presentation more shamefully than Russian sculler Vyacheslav Ivanov. He managed to lose his hard-earned medal just seconds after receiving it.

At the 1956 Melbourne Games, the eighteen-year-old Ivanov was competing in the single sculls on Lake Wendouree. No one expected the Soviet teen to do very well in his first taste of Olympic competition. But Ivanov made a sensational spurt with two hundred meters to go and beat out the two favorites. He crossed the finish line nearly five seconds ahead of Australian Stuart Mackenzie and more than nine seconds in front of third-place finisher Jack Kelly, Jr., brother of actress Grace Kelly. Jack had won every major single sculls title in the world except an Olympic gold medal.

The gold went to Ivanov, who was elated beyond belief. He clapped his hands and shouted with joy as he and the other medalists climbed onto a float moored to the dock where the awards ceremony was scheduled to take place immediately after the race.

The Boy Scouts carried the cherished medals down to the float for Avery Brundage, the president of the Olympic Federation, to present. As he handed Ivanov the gold medal, the thrilled young Russian jumped up and down with glee. But in all his happiness he didn't bother to get a firm hold on his cherished medal—and accidentally dropped it. The gold medallion fell right between two slats in the float and sank to the muddy bottom of Lake Wendouree.

The horrified klutz threw his hands up in grief and moaned in Russian, but Brundage tried to calm him by saying, "Never mind. I'll give you another one later." But Ivanov didn't want to wait for another one—he jumped into the water and tried to find his lost medal himself. After repeated dives into the shallow, five-foot-deep lake, the crushed Ivanov reluctantly gave up.

However, the next day, nearly three hundred Australian school children were mobilized to dive into Lake Wendouree in search of his medal. Although they scoured the underwater reeds and muddy bottom, they never found it.

"I know Ivanov wasn't happy, but it was a big ha-ha for us," recalled John Cook, a member of the United States eight-man rowing team who was at the awards ceremony. "There were some hard feelings against the Soviets at the time because of their invasion of Hungary. So we kept joking about how that dumb Russian beats Mackenzie and Kelly and then goes and drops his medal in the lake."

Whistle Stop

The Belgian soccer team lost its match against France because of a policeman's whistle.

During the 1960 Games in Rome, France and Belgium were battling in a scoreless tie when an Italian traffic cop, on duty just outside the field, blew his whistle with all his might at a reckless driver.

When the Belgians heard the loud whistle, they thought the umpire had blown it so they stopped playing. But the French didn't stop. Instead, they knocked the ball into the net for the only goal of the game.

Basketball Officials

In the worst miscarriage of justice in Olympic history, bumbling referees and a power-crazed courtside official cheated the U.S. basketball team out of the gold medal it had rightfully won.

The Americans had beaten the Soviet squad in regulation time, but astoundingly, officials gave the Russians two more opportunities to win. On the third—and illegal—try, the Soviets scored a last-second basket for an unbelievable 51–50 gold medal victory in the 1972 Games in Munich. It was the first defeat for an American Olympic basketball team, which had won sixty-two straight games since the sport first became an Olympic event in 1936.

In the final game against the Russians, the U.S. staged a valiant rally and trailed 49–48 when American Doug Collins picked up a loose ball at midcourt, drove for the basket, and was fouled with only three seconds left to play. Despite the crushing pressure, the Illinois State senior calmly sank both free throws to give the U.S. a dramatic 50–49 lead.

But then the officials stole the victory—and the gold medal—from the Americans when the Soviets were given three opportunities to score the winning basket.

The clock showed three seconds remaining when the Soviets inbounded the ball and it was deflected at midcourt. A crowd rushed onto the floor thinking the Americans had won. But referee Renato Righetto of Brazil blew his whistle when he saw the Russian coaches converge on the scorer's table, demanding a timeout. Two seconds had elapsed and the official clock showed one second remaining.

At this point, Great Britain's Dr. R. William Jones intervened. Jones, secretary-general of the International Amateur Basketball Federation (FIBA), ordered the clock set back to three seconds. Jones acted illegally because he had no right to make any rulings during a game; only the referees could do that. Nevertheless, Jones ruled FIBA with an iron hand, and no one dared question his authority.

For the second time, the Soviet team took the ball out of bounds, but Modestas Paulauskas' desperation shot was short. The horn sounded and the American players joined the crowd at midcourt, jubilant over their comeback and apparent victory. But their happiness was short-lived.

The clock had not been reset, and Jones, wielding power he didn't legally possess, ordered three seconds—not one second—again posted on the clock. Then he informed both coaches that the Soviet team would have one last play.

Hank Iba, the U.S. coach who had led American teams to gold medals in 1964 and 1968, angrily stalked after Jones and the referees and had to be restrained by his players before play began again.

The Soviet team made the most of its third chance to score. Tom McMillen, the 6-foot, 11-inch forward from Maryland, waved his arms to thwart the inbounds pass as he had done on the previous two attempts, but this time the referee ordered him to back off. When he did, Soviet player Ivan Yedeshko backed up, wound up, and threw the ball the length of the court to 6-foot, 8-inch Aleksander Belov. Americans Kevin Joyce and James Forbes went up for the ball with Belov, but he knocked them off balance with an obvious foul that wasn't called and then easily sank the ball one second before time expired for an incredible 51–50 victory.

Chaos ensued. Iba again rushed the scorer's table, Forbes wept unabashedly, and newsmen and irate fans flooded onto the floor. "I've never seen anything like this in all my years of basketball," Iba declared.

In the wild, closing seconds, the referees neglected to call two violations that were evident in the game films. One showed that Yedeshko had stepped on the baseline in making his full-court pass to Belov, which would have negated the scoring play and given the ball to the Americans.

The second oversight was equally flagrant—not calling a three-second violation against Belov. Under international rules, the three-second rule goes into effect once the official gives the ball to the player out of bounds, not when the clock begins. The refs failed to notice that Belov had stationed himself inside the three-second lane for at least five seconds.

The official result of the game was delayed because Hank Iba filed a protest that was considered by a five-man FIBA Jury of Appeals made up of members from Cuba, Poland, Puerto Rico, Hungary, and Italy. It was a kangaroo court because the members from the three Soviet-bloc nations—Cuba, Poland, and Hungary—naturally upheld the Russians' victory while the minority—the Italian and Puerto Rican representatives—voted to disallow Belov's basket.

The U.S. team had a vote of their own—they decided unanimously to refuse their silver medals because they had been robbed of their victory.

Hank Iba was doubly victimized. First, he was fleeced out of the gold medal. Then, while he was arguing with officials at courtside after the game, Iba's wallet, containing $370, was filched. "They've even taken to picking my pockets," the coach lamented in the locker room. "What else can go wrong?"

Trying to Slide By

The East German women's luge (otherwise known as toboggan) team discovered the secret to winning—cheat.

At the 1968 Games in Grenoble, France, East Germans Ortrun Enderlein, Anna-Maria Muller, and Angela Knosel finished first, second, and fourth respectively. However, the women aroused suspicion because they always showed up for their runs at the last minute and left as soon as they had finished their run.

The sledders were disqualified and buried in an avalanche of shame when an investigation revealed that they illegally heated the runners of their luges over an open fire in a sneaky attempt to obtain greater speed.

Allen Warren   David Hunt

Yachting ■ Montreal Games ■ July, 1976

The most shameful Olympic flame in history blazed not from a torch but from a burning boat—in a fire deliberately set by its two-man crew.

Skipper Allen Warren and his mate David Hunt, both Britishers, were racing their six-year-old keelboat *Gift 'Orse* in the Tempest Class in the 1976 Olympic yachting competition on Lake Ontario. But on the circuitous course, their boat slipped farther and farther behind the rest of the fleet.

Finally, Warren and Hunt decided to give up not only the race but the poorly performing boat as well. So the yachtsmen took some acetone and a flare and set their boat on fire! The flames prompted a Canadian destroyer to come to the rescue of the British crew, but Warren just waved it away.

"We're quite all right," the forty-one-year-old skipper told the Navy. "We always sail like this." But when the smoke began obscuring the finish line, the destroyer returned and picked up the Britishers. Then the big ship put the *Gift 'Orse* out of its misery by ramming it. Down went the stricken boat as the lake waters extinguished the flames.

"She went lame on us so we decided the poor old *'Orse* should be cremated," said Warren, who back on land was a funeral director. "It wasn't worth taking her all the way back home. We wanted to give her a proper Viking funeral."

Added his mate, "My skipper has style, but not that much. I tried to persuade him to burn with the ship, but he wouldn't agree."

Boris Onischenko

Modern Pentathlon ■ Montreal Games ■ July, 1976

Five events make up the modern pentathlon—horse riding, fencing, shooting, swimming, and cross-country running. Boris Onischenko added a new event—cheating.

The Russian was an international competitor of long standing who excelled in fencing. He had thrust and parried his way to one gold and two silver medals in previous Olympiads. Dazzling spectators with his catlike quickness, Boris repeatedly lit up the light over the judges' desk. (Each fencer is wired so that when his épée, or dueling sword, makes proper contact with his opponent, a blinking light registers a hit.) Onischenko was so fast that often his hits couldn't even be seen. That's because they weren't really hits.

During the 1976 Summer Olympics in Montreal, the judges were en garde when Boris took to the floor for his fencing duel on the second day of the five-day modern pentathlon. At first, the judges assumed his épée was defective because the indicator light was flashing before the weapon touched his opponent. But on closer inspection, they discovered that his foil had not been broken, but had been tampered with. The weapon was wired so that it would score a winning hit without making contact.

Onischenko insisted that his foil was faulty. The only thing faulty was his lame excuse. The Jury of Appeals stuck it to Boris by banning him from the Olympics on the grounds that he had cheated. The disqualified Russian was forced to fly home in disgrace.

The only question left unanswered was whether he had used the rigged foil to win those gold and silver medals in previous Olympiads.

Onischenko, after judges stuck it to him   AP/Wide World Photos

THE BOWLING HALL OF SHAME

Palmer Fallgren

Cougar Open ■ March 20, 1971

The wildest ball ever thrown in a pro tournament wasn't a gutter ball. It was a *ceiling* ball.

Palmer Fallgren, then a nineteen-year-old bowler in his second year on the pro tour, literally hit the ceiling with his ball during the Cougar Open at the Madison Square Garden Bowling Center.

"I've never had a more embarrassing moment," said Fallgren. "People still come up to me on the tour and ask if it's really true."

It happened in the eighth frame after the then young temperamental bowler left a 4–6 split. "I was so ticked off that I didn't even wait for my ball to get back," Fallgren recalled. "I had another ball, so I just grabbed that instead, stared at the split, and then tried to throw the ball as hard as I could."

In his haste and fury, Fallgren forgot about the tape that he had placed in the finger holes of his spare ball before the tourney. When he tried to release the ball on his follow-through, the ball stuck to his fingers for just a second. Instead of rolling the ball straight *down* the alley, Fallgren launched the ball straight *up*.

The 6-foot, 1-inch, 170-pound bowler threw with such forceful anger that his sixteen-pound ball smashed into the fifteen-foot-high ceiling. Then it plunged back down to the alley with a reverberating bang about ten feet in front of the foul line, rolled down the lane— and knocked down the 4 pin!

"I went into total shock," said Fallgren. "It was so embarrassing, I didn't know what to do or what to say. When the ball hit the floor, it sounded like a cannonball and the bowlers on all the other lanes just stopped right in their tracks. I was frozen, too, just staring at the ceiling. I couldn't believe what I had done."

Although the 4 pin was toppled, the rules of bowling disallowed the knockdown. Afterward, officials told Fallgren he was being fined $100 for "a shot unbecoming a professional." However, after all these years, he has yet to pay it.

Fallgren's throw left quite an impression not only on his fellow bowlers but on the ceiling and alley as well.

"He put a dent in the ceiling and it's still there today," said Tom

Fallgren, the only pro to hit the ceiling   Professional Bowlers Association

Roballey, director of the bowling center. "He also dented the lane and we had to put down new wood.

"It could have been a lot worse. When Fallgren's ball hit the ceiling, it missed a sprinkler head by just three inches. Our building engineer told me that if the ball had struck the sprinkler head, we would have been flooded out."

Don Genalo

Southern California Open ■ June 11, 1983

Don Genalo was on his way to chalking up his third Professional Bowlers Association tournament win of the year.

But in the last frame of the final game, he was disgusted with himself because he left an almost impossible 4-6-7-9-10 "Greek church" split. Thinking he had blown the match, the dejected Genalo halfheartedly tossed his next ball without looking and it landed in the gutter.

It was only then he discovered that he had needed to knock down only three of the five pins left standing in the split to salvage victory. Instead, Genalo lost 214–212.

"It was just a real inexcusable, stupid mistake on my part," Genalo admitted as he recalled his costly gaffe at the Southern California Open at the Gable House Lanes in Torrance, California.

"Jimmie Pritts was my opponent in the final," recounted the third-year pro. "He was bowling really well and I figured that if he threw a strike, I'd have to double out to win. Jimmie left a 10 pin on his first shot and then picked it up for a spare. But I still had it locked in my head that I needed a double. I even checked the score sheet, but I added wrong.

"I threw a strike and the crowd cheered. I concentrated on my next shot, thinking I needed that second strike to win. But I made an absolutely atrocious shot and left the 'Greek church' split and I thought I had lost. I figured the next roll didn't mean a thing, so I just threw the ball down there and it landed in the gutter. I told myself that it was no big deal. Little did I know how big a deal it really was.

"I was getting ready to congratulate Jimmie when somebody said, 'What a shame to have lost by just two pins like that.' When I found out I had added the score wrong, I wanted to bounce off the walls. I was ready to blow up the building with me in it."

Had Genalo realized that he was only two pins behind, he would easily have picked up three of the five pins left standing on his next roll. He also would have picked up an additional $5,500—the difference in prize money between first and second place.

"It hurts to talk about it, but there's no way I can pretend it didn't happen, especially when millions of people saw it," he said. "You see, ABC was televising the finals nationally. It was all so stupid and embarrassing."

Agony of De Feet

If only Henry Starkey hadn't been so excited, he might have rolled his first perfect game.

In the first nine frames of a league game in Alexandria, Virginia, in 1982, Henry threw nine strikes. On his tenth delivery, it looked like he lost his bid for a 300 game when he left a solid 7 pin. But luckily another pin rolled into the 7 and knocked it over.

The joyous Henry jumped so high that when he landed, he sprained his left ankle. Even though he was in pain, he insisted on hobbling to the line on one foot with friends on both sides of him holding him up. Rolling the ball from a weird hop-step delivery, Henry saw his dream of a perfect game vanish when he knocked down only six pins. But he still managed to smile through his heart-ache and pain. He picked up his spare on the next ball and finished with a 286—still his highest game ever.

Dick Weber

All-Star Tournament ▪ December 9, 1956

In 1956, pro bowling had finally made it big. For the first time ever, the All-Star Tournament—the World Series of bowling—was being telecast over national television.

The network cameras were in place at the Coliseum in Chicago for the showdown between the then world's two best bowlers—Dick Weber and Don Carter. Announcer Whispering Joe Wilson opened the telecast to the cheers of a capacity crowd of 2,000.

Then the spectators hushed as Weber—the leading money-winner of his time—got set to roll the first ball ever on network television. As he stepped onto the lane, Dick thought, "What better way to open this historic moment than with a strike?" He was the bowler who could do just that, having racked up twenty-three perfect games in his great career.

Making a picture-perfect approach, Weber let loose his ball as the audience at home and at the alley waited for the pins to fly. But the ball never made it that far.

Dick Weber—the bowlers' bowler who was the only pro to win major championships in four different decades—had opened bowling's first national televised tournament by throwing a gutter ball!

"That was the most embarrassing moment in my life, no doubt about it," admitted Weber, a member of the Bowling Hall of Fame. "I'm glad we didn't have color TV in those days because my face was sure red—beet red.

"Everybody was all excited about being on national television for the first time. I wanted to get on with it, but we had to wait a few minutes until Whispering Joe Wilson finished with his opening. The wait might have made me a little nervous.

"As the first one up, I naturally wanted to throw a good ball. On my release, the ball always came pretty close to my ankle, and wouldn't you know that this time my ball hit my ankle and went right into the gutter—while the whole world was watching.

"Carter didn't say anything to me. He was a gentleman about it and looked the other way, but I could still see that he had a little grin on his face."

But Tom Hennessey, a teammate of Dick's on the Budweiser pro bowling team, wasn't about to remain silent over Weber's embarrassing blunder. Between frames, Hennessey went up to him and whispered, "Dick, we know Carter is going to win anyway, but you don't have to make it look so easy for him."

Richard Caplette

September 7, 1971

If there is a hell for bowlers, Richard Caplette is a charter member. No one ever rolled a more deplorable game in league competition than he did.

During one horrendous and unforgettable night, Caplette, who owned a creditable 170 average, set the American Bowling Congress record for the lowest score in league play—an incredible 3! Not only that, but he also established a black mark for most gutter balls in a single game—nineteen!

The pins could have been as big as sequoias and it wouldn't have made any difference. Caplette simply couldn't hit them. He ended up in the gutter more times than a Skid Row drunk.

"No matter what I tried, I just couldn't keep the ball on the alley," recalled Caplette, who lives in Danielson, Connecticut. "The biggest mistake I made that night was showing up at the bowling alley."

It was the opener of the new bowling season and Caplette was rolling for the VFW team at the Friendly Bowl in nearby Brooklyn, Connecticut. He felt good and hoped to shoot a 200 game. By the end of the evening, he discovered that his expectations were off by 197 pins.

Caplette's first inclination that this was not going to be his night came early when he knocked down only three pins on his first ball and rolled his second ball in the gutter. He muttered and cursed. But had Caplette known what misfortune lay ahead, he probably would have cheered, because that was the only frame in which he managed to score!

"I couldn't stop throwing gutter balls," he said. "I kept doing it frame after frame. Our scores were posted overhead and that didn't help, especially since our team bowled in a lane right next to the women's league. After each gutter ball, I'd sit down and a different woman would come over and say, 'Can I help you?' That was bad enough. But then about the seventh frame, the president of our league hollered over to our team captain, 'Hey, Duke. Who do you have on your team tonight? A blind bowler?' I was ready to give up then, but I went ahead and finished.

"I was really trying my best, too. I wasn't drunk or anything like that. It was just that the harder I tried, the worse I got. I never saw anything like it in my life."

Neither had anyone else. Of the twenty balls he rolled, nineteen were consecutive gutter balls—an ABC record for futile consistency.

Caplette, who lives only two miles away from the Friendly Bowl, says he has never set foot in the place since that awful night. He even worked on the roof of the bowling alley—but he wouldn't go inside. "I just never went back," he admitted. "I completely gave up bowling after that. I never threw another ball. I was too embarrassed to show my face around an alley again."

Fran Wolf

Dayton Classic ■ July 20, 1976

One of the worst fears bowlers have is that the ball will fly off behind them on the backswing. Third-year women's pro Fran Wolf realized this fear not once, not twice, but *four* times in one tournament.

"It's a memory that will stay with me forever," laughed Fran, now tournament director for the Ladies Professional Bowling Tour. "I lost my ball on my practice throw in each of the four rounds of the Dayton Classic. I'll never forget where it happened because it was at the Beaverview Bowl. What a name to hold a women's tournament!

"Anyway, the first time I did it, the ball flew out of my hand behind me and crashed with a loud bang that silenced the whole place. That was embarrassing, but it got worse. In the second round, I lost my ball on the backswing again. I had hoped no one saw me, but naturally everyone had. I didn't know what to do, so I kicked my ball back toward the settee [sitting area].

"When I got up for my practice ball in the third round, I just knew it was going to happen again, so I marched up there and told myself, 'Well, let's get this over with.' Sure enough, the ball flew out of my hand on the backswing."

For the fourth round, Fran was in the finals, so she was in the spotlight more than ever. She was hoping that everyone had forgotten about her wild practice throws. They hadn't. As Fran walked up to the lane, she glanced back. There, standing on the settees seeking safety, were her competitors. Faced with such a show of no confidence, Fran knew she was doomed. For the fourth time in a row, she lost her grip on her practice ball and it sailed behind her, landing on the wood with a thwack. "When I turned around, everyone was applauding," she recalled. "It was the biggest applause I got during the whole tournament."

At least Fran didn't fling the most shameful practice ball. That dishonor goes to ten-time national tournament winner Vesma Grinfelds. During the 1975 Women's International Bowling Congress tourney in Las Vegas, Vesma was determined to get off to a good start by firing a practice strike. She did, too. But not at the pins. Vesma lost control of her ball on the backswing and it soared out of her hand backward and crashed right into the settee!

"I casually went over to the settee," recalled Vesma, "and calmly picked up my ball and said, 'Well, that's my practice throw.' "

Mark Baker

Miami Miller Lite Tournament ■ February 4, 1984

Pro bowler Mark Baker suffered the most embarrassing split ever in a tournament—when the seat of his pants ripped open.

The third-year pro revealed a new side of himself during the Miami Miller Lite tourney at Don Carter Lanes in the suburb of Kendall Lakes.

"I needed to get a strike in the tenth frame to beat my opponent, so I was psyched," Baker recalled. "I put something extra in my throw and I went down to one knee on the follow-through. Then I heard my pants rip.

"I didn't think much of it because I got my strike and I was really pumped up. But the crowd—it was standing room only—let me know immediately. When I heard a woman spectator say, 'My, what a white ass he has,' I reached behind me and discovered a huge hole in the seat of my pants. Being from California, I wasn't a big believer in underwear, so my bare butt was hanging out for all to see."

The red-faced Baker immediately excused himself, pulled out his bowling shirt so the shirt tail would cover up his torn pants, and walked through the tittering crowd to the locker room to change. "I was never so embarrassed," he recalled, "especially when everyone gave me a standing ovation." After changing pants, Baker just wanted to put the matter behind him. He returned to finish the tenth frame and barely beat out his opponent.

"The next day, everyone started calling me 'Moon.' I appeared on a televised tournament and the sportscaster told the TV audience what had happened to me and my pants. The following week, I received seventeen pairs of underwear in the mail from various women across the country."

Alley Oops!

Lowlights from the American Bowling Congress Record Book

- Most fouls in a league game—15
  Bud Mathieson, Ocean Beach, California, December 30, 1946
- Most gutter balls in a league season—89
  Poodles Nelson, Defender Club, New York, New York, 1895–96.
- Consecutive losses in league play—120
  Downes Construction Co., Moravia, New York, 1965–66 (96 losses) and 1966–67 (24 losses)
- Most consecutive 7–10 splits in a game—6
  Payne Rose, St. Louis, Missouri, September, 1962

THE BOXING
HALL OF SHAME

Joseph "Ace" Falu

Junior Middleweight ▪ New York ▪ February 26, 1962

Ace Falu achieved boxing infamy in only fourteen seconds.

Falu, a twenty-two-year-old amateur boxer who had fought in New York City's Spanish Golden Gloves, decided to turn pro. Harboring no dreamy expectations about being a contender, Ace merely wanted to earn enough money as a prizefighter to open a small grocery store.

In his pro debut at the old St. Nicholas Arena in Manhattan, Ace went up against Norman Cassaberry, a junior middleweight with only a few pro wins under his belt. Ace was pumped up for the bout, eager to throw his best punches, and ready to take his opponent's best shots.

When the bell rang for the first round, Ace showed the same sportsmanship he displayed as an amateur. He came out with his hands extended to touch gloves with Cassaberry. But since this was a fight and not a social, Cassaberry skipped the amenities. He tossed a left followed by a powerful right to the chin, knocking Ace to the canvas seven seconds into the round. By the count of seven, Ace courageously staggered to his feet, but referee George Coyle could see the dazed boxer was in no condition to fight and halted the bout.

The punches knocked out any further boxing ambitions for Ace. He decided then and there to quit for good. But at least he left the ring with a record—the shortest pro career in the history of prize fighting. Fourteen seconds.

Jitterbug Smith

Lightweight ▪ New Orleans ▪ September 8, 1958

Jitterbug Smith kayoed his opponent—yet still managed to get *himself* counted out.

Jitterbug was pounding the daylights out of Ralph Espinia in the first two rounds of a lightweight bout in New Orleans. When the bell sounded for the next round, Jitterbug knew he had the fight won and toyed with his outclassed foe for another minute. Then Jitterbug delivered a crushing right to the jaw that turned out the lights for Espinia, who toppled to the canvas.

Jitterbug smiled, figuring he had won the fight. All he had to do was amble over to a neutral corner and watch referee Pete Giarusso count out the fallen Espinia. But Jitterbug didn't do that. Apparently, one of Espinia's weak punches had knocked the smarts out of him, because Jitterbug stupidly sat down in the ring, as if he were sunning himself at the beach, and waited for the knockout to be official.

Giarusso counted ten over Espinia—but at the same time counted ten over Jitterbug. Since the relaxing boxer wasn't on his feet, he was considered kayoed, too.

When the crowd stopped laughing over the rare double knock-out, the shocked Jitterbug took one final swing—this one aimed at the boxing rules. "This is too much!" declared Jitterbug, who then announced he was retiring from the ring.

Jack Welsh

Referee ■ World Lightweight Championship Bout ■ July 4, 1912

Referee Jack Welsh dealt boxing the most outrageously low blow ever in the history of the sport by turning the world lightweight championship bout into a sham.

When both fighters were floored by simultaneous knockdown punches, the palooka of a referee counted out the challenger—while at the same time helping the dazed champion to his feet and declaring him the winner!

In the thirteenth round of the fierce title fight between champ Ad Wolgast and challenger Joe Rivers, both boxers were trading punches, their faces puffed and cut. Near the end of the stanza, Wolgast sent a right to the body and followed with a wicked left below the belt at the very moment he himself was struck with an equally powerful blow to the jaw.

Rivers crashed to the floor and Wolgast fell on top of him as both men groaned in agony. Wolgast struggled wearily to a sitting position, but he had been knocked too silly to stand. Meanwhile, Rivers was sprawled full length on the canvas, holding his groin with both hands as his frantic cornermen screamed foul.

Faced with a bizarre double knockdown, Welsh stared at the fallen fighters for several seconds, wondering if either would get up.

Welsh about to commit ring robbery   Courtesy The Ring Magazine

When neither did, he decided to take matters into his own hands. The 11,000 fans at the Vernon Arena near Los Angeles were aghast and infuriated at what they saw next. With his left hand, Welsh lifted the punch-drunk champ to his feet and with his right hand, the ref counted out the prone challenger. As if that weren't a raw enough deal, Welsh shortchanged Rivers with a quick count that was completed a split second after the bell ended the round.

Timekeeper Al Holder shouted that he had rung the gong but Welsh paid him no heed. Rivers, his face contorted in agony, struggled to his feet unaided and squared away, ready to renew the battle. However, Welsh waved him to his corner and declared Wolgast was still champion. Wolgast was too dazed to realize that he had won. He tottered around the ring in pain and then fainted and had to be carried back to his dressing room.

The arena erupted in bedlam. Rivers's cornermen surrounded Welsh and screamed in protest as irate fans stormed the ring and shouted, "Robbery! Robbery!" Welsh then tried to leave the ring but was stopped by boxing promoter and attorney Earl Rogers. "It's the most gigantic wholesale swindle ever!" shouted Rogers. Hearing enough swearing to get a cauliflower ear, Welsh somehow managed to weasel through the incensed crowd and dashed out of the arena.

"It was the worst case of robbery in the history of the American ring," declared Rivers's manager, Joe Levy. "Never before have I seen a referee pick up a man and then give him the decision. The foul blow struck by Wolgast was seen by every man near ringside." To back up his claim of a low blow, Rivers showed the newsmen in his dressing room his dented aluminum protective cup.

Later, Welsh defended his actions by saying he made a difficult judgment call. The truth is, the ref did some fancy footwork to toy with the rules and give a break to one of his closest friends—who happened to be none other than Ad Wolgast.

Muhammad Ali

World Heavyweight Champion ■ Tokyo ■ June 26, 1976

Muhammad Ali's fighting credo was "float like a butterfly, sting like a bee." But in a shameful ring performance not befitting a champion, Ali did nothing but float like a rock, sting like a moth.

For $6 million, the world's most popular, wealthiest heavyweight boxing champion accepted the absurd challenge of Japanese wrestler Kanji Antonio Inoki to a fifteen-round bout in Tokyo. Ballyhooed by promoters as "The War of the Worlds," Ali turned the fight into the bore of the ages.

It was, in fact, the dullest sporting event ever televised—a rip-off for the millions of fans throughout the world who watched this fiasco on closed-circuit TV.

They saw Ali throw only six punches in the entire fight. That's a million bucks a punch. He landed only two harmless jabs. Meanwhile, Inoki scooted around the ring on his back like a crab with his belly up. From this position he kept kicking the champ in the leg, hoping to down Ali while still keeping his own chin out of the boxer's reach.

Inoki, whose prominent jaw earned him the nickname Pelican, kicked Ali about sixty times in the leg. The champ's shin was bloodied and the back of his leg was covered with hematomas. His corner worked on the leg early, applying ice bags and Vaseline. Had the injury become worse, it could have been the first bout ever stopped because of a leg cut.

For his part, Ali clowned, stuck his tongue out, and gestured to Inoki to stand up and punch with him. But Ali managed always to stay

Ali In "Bore of the Worlds"   UPI/Bettmann Newsphotos

close to the ropes because the rules said that he could stop the action—as if there was any—by simply grabbing the ropes.

Whenever Inoki tried to kick Ali's legs out from under him, the champ moved to a corner and lifted himself onto the ropes. Often during the match, the combatants motioned to each other to come closer. Ali at times did a hula, patted Inoki's backside, and waved mockingly at him.

The "fight" between the thirty-four-year-old boxer and the thirty-three-year-old son of a Japanese farmer ended to no one's satisfaction in a draw. The farce was so boring that many of the 14,000 fans at the Japan Martial Arts Hall tossed trash into the ring at the end of the last round.

The Ali-Inoki travesty was supposed to settle once and for all that age-old barroom question: Who would win a match between a wrestler and a boxer? One thing was answered. We know who would lose. The fans.

Yankee Sullivan

American Heavyweight Championship Bout ■ October 12, 1853

In the craziest TKO in ring history, heavyweight boxer Yankee Sullivan was ruled the loser for failing to answer the call to fight—because he was too busy beating up his opponent's cornermen!

In front of thousands of shouting, wagering fans at Boston Four Corners, Massachusetts, Sullivan duked it out in a gory, exhausting bare-knuckle bout with challenger John C. Morrissey. The boxers fought furiously from the start, although Sullivan did the most damage. By the fifth round, Morrissey's left eye was swollen shut and his face and chest were smeared with blood. Yet Yankee couldn't put him away.

The grueling battle raged on and on. Sullivan still held the upper hand, making Morrissey's face resemble a piece of raw beefsteak. By the end of the thirty-sixth round, Morrissey's knees trembled with weakness, his eyes glazed with pain.

At the start of the thirty-seventh round, Yankee tried to finish his opponent off with some hit-and-run boxing. But Morrissey pursued, threw his arms around Sullivan, and lifted him off his feet against the ropes.

Outraged by these devious tactics, Yankee's seconds rushed into the ring and to his aid. Meanwhile, Morrissey's cornermen charged onto the canvas to make sure that no harm came to their man. Within seconds, the fans were watching a new, unscheduled—and altogether shameful—fight between the boxers' handlers.

Morrissey was smart enough to disentangle himself from the brawlers and return to his corner. Sullivan was not so wise. He joined the melee and was punching the challenger's second, Awful Gardner, when referee Charley Allaire demanded that the two boxers get back to fighting each other.

Morrissey stepped to the center of the ring with his fists upraised. But Sullivan paid no heed to the ref's call because, across the way, he was still slugging it out with Morrissey's men. After Yankee ignored Allaire's repeated orders to resume the bout, the ref was left with no other choice. He proclaimed Morrissey the winner by a TKO.

Thus, Morrissey became the American heavyweight champion only because his opponent was too busy fighting someone else.

Mike DeCosmo   Laurie Buxton

Welterweights ■ Newark ■ May 18, 1948

For ten rounds, welterweights Mike DeCosmo and Laurie Buxton threw a flurry of punches, but neither could deck the other. Nevertheless, each recorded a KO—they knocked out the referee!

Fans at the Meadowbrook Bowl in Newark were treated to a close fight between DeCosmo, the local favorite, and Buxton, an Englishman. As the last few seconds of the match ticked off, the boxers finished with a flourish, belting away at each other toe-to-toe. They were now fighting with such intensity that they failed to hear the bell sound, ending the tenth and final round.

Referee Joe Walker then stepped between the two flailing boxers and tried to separate them. Instead, they separated him from his consciousness when they simultaneously walloped him on the chin with blows that left him flat on his back.

It took a minute before the ref was revived on the canvas with a few whiffs of ammonia. Walker, whose brother Mickey was a middleweight and welterweight champ, showed why he could never follow in Mickey's footsteps—he couldn't take a punch (or in this case, two punches).

After staggering to his feet, Walker—wincing in pain over his sore chin, torn mouth, and chipped tooth—gave the decision to Buxton. Angered DeCosmo fans then shouted that Walker should have stayed down for the count.

Referee Walker taking the count   AP/Wide World Photos

The Canvas Always Looks Whiter on the Other Side of the Ropes

While fighting middleweight champ Sugar Ray Robinson, Maxie Shapiro kept his wit but lost his confidence.

In the second round of a bout in New York on September 19, 1941, Robinson caught Shapiro with a hook that sent him through the ropes and onto the apron of the ring. Maxie got up but stayed on the apron with his arms draped across the top rope, trying to clear his head.

Just then, a fan yelled at Shapiro, "Hey, Maxie, you're on the wrong side of the ropes!"

Shapiro turned around and shouted back, "That's what you think!" He was knocked out in the next round.

Kenneth Harper vs. Rocky Scarfone

Welterweight Bout ■ Miami Beach ■ April 15, 1980

The only thing square about the welterweight bout between Kenneth Harper and Rocky Scarfone was the ring. Their fight would have been totally forgettable if it hadn't been for the ludicrous way it ended.

Harper, then nineteen, was making his professional debut against Scarfone, a local favorite and proven "ticket seller." To the surprise of many in the Miami Beach crowd, Harper came out smoking and broke Scarfone's nose and cut his mouth in the first two rounds. Before the start of the third round, referee Eddie Eckert called in ringside physician Robert LaVey to examine the battered Scarfone, whose face was covered with blood.

In the opposite corner, a confident, pumped-up Harper was wondering if his hurt opponent would be able to answer the bell for the next round. As he watched Dr. LaVey enter the ring, Harper figured the physician would stop the fight.

Dr. LaVey began walking toward Scarfone but then suddenly detoured and headed for Harper. Rather than examine the bloodied Scarfone, the doctor checked Harper instead. LaVey found two of the boxer's lower teeth had been chipped and, with a perfectly straight face, announced that Harper could not continue. Incredibly, the badly beaten Scarfone was declared the winner by a TKO!

Even more outrageous, the Miami Beach Boxing Commission refused to investigate the fight at first. But there was such an uproar from fans and the press that the commission finally held a hearing. LaVey testified that Harper's manager Emmett Sullivan had called him over to look at the boxer's chipped teeth. "The kid quit," said LaVey. "He asked me to stop it. He told me, 'I got enough. I don't want no more.'" But Harper testified, "Why would I say anything like that? I would have had the guy in the next round." He insisted that the fight had been stopped against his will. When the hearing was over, the commission refused to take any action.

Said Harry Brennen, who saw the fight before becoming a member of the Florida State Athletic Commission, "I think the people involved in the fight got mixed up and misread the script."

What middleweight champ TKO'd a referee?

Sugar Ray Leonard. On October 6, 1978, Leonard was battling Randy Shields when referee Tom Kelly carelessly got in the way of a wicked Leonard hook in Round 9 that split open Kelly's eye and turned his legs to jelly. He had to be replaced for the tenth and final round by a substitute. Leonard was given the decision over Shields—and credited with an unofficial TKO over referee Kelly.

Otto Nispel

Referee ■ Sugar Ray Robinson–Gerhard Hecht Bout
Berlin ■ June 24, 1951

Sugar Ray Robinson knocked out his opponent twice—yet was declared the loser!

The real loser was referee Otto Nispel, who officiated a scheduled ten-round nontitle bout in Berlin between Robinson, then the world middleweight champion, and German challenger Gerhard Hecht.

Midway through the first round, Robinson caught Hecht with a hard left hook which sent the German to the canvas. As Hecht writhed in obvious pain, Nispel counted to nine. Then, instead of completing the count, the German ref had the unmitigated gall to announce an unprecedented one-minute pause! Seconds later, the bell rang ending the round. Hecht staggered to his corner and collapsed on his stool as his seconds feverishly worked to revive him.

Hecht, plainly outclassed by Sugar Ray, reluctantly came out for the second round. But it was no contest. Robinson quickly closed in on his prey and hammered Hecht with a series of lightning punches. For the second time, the German hit the canvas, unable to get up.

Robinson returned to his corner to wait for the ten-count and the raising of his hand. But to Ray's shock, Nispel halted the bout and announced that Robinson had been disqualified for throwing illegal kidney punches.

Stunned beyond belief, Sugar Ray angrily confronted the ref and declared, "What's the matter with you? You know that wasn't a foul!" Nispel murmured, "I have to call it a foul. I want to leave this ring alive."

By now, the 25,000 German fans who crowded into the Waldbuehne, an open-air amphitheater, took up the cry, "Foul! Foul! Foul!" Then they hurled bottles and garbage into the ring. The champ's handlers hustled him under the elevated ring where dozens of sportswriters were already huddled. Police promptly battled their way through the angry throng to deliver Robinson to the safety of his dressing room.

Nispel's ruling was so blatantly ridiculous that the very next day the West Berlin Boxing Commission set aside Sugar Ray's disqualification and ruled "no decision" for the riotous two-round fight. A day after that announcement, the commission suspended Nispel for three months.

Edouard Rabret, general secretary of the European Boxing Union, summed up the feeling of boxing fans everywhere when he told the world press, "The second round was a farce—as was Nispel's decision."

Ralph Walton

Welterweight ■ Lewiston, Maine ■ September 23, 1946

It was bad enough getting knocked out in the first round, but Ralph Walton added insult to his own injury by setting a record for the quickest KO in boxing—ten and a half seconds!

Walton, a 142-pound welterweight from Montreal, was in his corner getting last-minute instructions from his handlers before his fight with local boxer Al "Shiner" Couture. The bout was a scheduled ten-rounder, the main event on the card at the City Hall auditorium in Lewiston, Maine.

Walton, who had a three-pound advantage over his opponent, was eager to box. But he wasn't nearly as eager as Couture. At least a second or two before the bell signaled the start of the fight, Couture dashed across the ring.

Neither Walton nor his handlers noticed him. One of Walton's seconds was standing outside the ropes on the apron adjusting the boxer's mouthpiece when the bell rang.

Walton took his hands off the ropes and turned around, expecting to see Couture coming out of the opposite corner. To his shock, he found himself toe-to-toe with his adversary. Before Walton could react, Courture greeted him with a powerful punch to the solar plexus. He went down in a heap.

Referee Tom Breen counted Walton out, ending the fight a record ten and a half seconds after it began. Asked later if Couture was a good fighter, Walton reportedly said, "I don't know. I wasn't in the ring long enough to find out."

Putting Down Their Dukes

It was the dullest round in boxing history.

On May 11, 1871, in Ontario, Jem Mace and Joe Coburn squared off for a bare-knuckle bout. In those days, a round ended only when a fighter slipped or was knocked down.

Within minutes, the 1,500 spectators began booing because neither boxer would box. Coburn wanted to fight against the ropes in his corner while Mace preferred to mix it up in the center of the ring. Neither would give in. "At times, the men stood contemplating one another for as much as five minutes without raising their arms," wrote one reporter.

Round 1 lasted one hour and nine minutes without either fighter laying a solid fist on the other. It would have lasted indefinitely had it not been broken up by the police.

The Gong Show

More Absurd Moments in Ring History

• 1920—Referee Jack McAuliffe forgets how to count to ten. In first round, Jimmy O'Gatty floors Packey McFarland four times. But each time, ref allows McFarland to get up without count. After McFarland is sent to canvas for fifth time, McAuliffe again refuses to count and waits for boxer to arise. After nearly ten minutes, ref finally remembers how to count and declares McFarland kayoed.

• 1934—Cornermen nearly swoon from smelly blanket. While getting into ring for last time, lightweight contender Billy "Fargo Express" Petrolle wears generations-old family Indian blanket around shoulders as he had whenever he entered arena during ten-year boxing career. Billy's handlers gag when climbing into corner because robe has never been washed and stinks worse than skunk. Petrolle believes robe's luck would wash down drain with suds.

• 1940—Welterweight fight ends in brawl with police. Welterweights Fritzie Zivic and Al "Bummy" Davis engage in cuffing, heeling, gouging, and elbowing. After tenth foul blow is struck by Davis, referee Bill Cavanaugh disqualifies Davis but boxers continue to fight. Cornermen and police rush into ring and pull furiously struggling combatants apart as crowd spits, curses, and throws objects at Davis.

• 1952—Referee kayoed by irate boxer. In German middleweight bout in Cologne, Peter Mueller gets so irked by referee Max Pippow's officiating that he suddenly attacks Pippow without warning and slugs him to canvas. German Boxing Association promptly bans Mueller for life.

• 1966—Roberto Duran horses around. Lightweight champ Roberto Duran earns first money with fists as teen in bet at town fair in native Panama. Bettors claim there is one opponent at fair who can take Duran's best shot and still remain standing. For $10, Duran takes bet, delivers shattering right to head. Down goes his opponent—a horse!

Alan Minter Fans

London ■ September 27, 1980

Seconds after Marvin Hagler battered England's Alan Minter for the undisputed middleweight championship of the world, the winner had an even bigger fight on his hands—with the crowd.

Minter's fans created such terror that Hagler couldn't even be proclaimed the new champ. Instead, he had to be smuggled out of the ring for his own safety.

Hagler—accompanied by a contingent of two dozen of his townsfolk from Brockton, Massachusetts—traveled to London determined to take the title away from Minter, a revered national celebrity in England.

In front of 10,000 beer-swilling, rowdy Britons at Wembley Arena, Hagler pummeled their hero. Midway through the third round, Minter was dazed and bleeding so badly from deep cuts under both eyes that the fight was stopped.

Hagler immediately dropped to his knees and raised his arms in celebration. But before he could get up, he was met with a barrage of beer bottles—many of them half-full—launched by a howling, ugly mob. When the flying missiles began whistling toward Hagler, his handlers turned from celebrants to bodyguards. They hastily leaped

Hagler dealing with blood, sweat, and beers   UPI/Bettmann Newsphotos into the ring and formed a human shell to take the brunt of the attack and protect the besieged boxer. Hagler's trainer and manager, Goody Petronelli, was hit by a bottle. Quickly, helmeted bobbies moved in and, along with the cornermen, formed a phalanx to herd Hagler safely through the ropes. The murderous crowd wouldn't let them get to the dressing room, so they hustled into a tunnel under the balcony and straight to the arena's police security headquarters.

During the height of this London blitz, brave ringside reporters and broadcasters carried on by holding their chairs over their heads.

"I was scared and panicking," Petronelli said later to the press. "I'd been warned that we'd hear a lot of noise, but I never expected the bottle throwing. Not in England. And then, when we finally got to our limo, they had smashed the windshield. Thank God we weren't in it then."

It was a tainted night for Hagler, a disastrous one for Minter, and a shameful moment for England.

Henry Wallitsch

Heavyweight ■ Long Island ■ September 12, 1959

Henry Wallitsch was knocked out by his own worst enemy—himself!

Wallitsch, of New York, was a free-swinging 189-pound heavyweight who was seeking revenge on his opponent, 175-pound Bartolo Soni of the Dominican Republic. Six weeks earlier, Soni had scored a split decision over Wallitsch.

Early in their scheduled ten-round rematch at the Island Garden Arena on Long Island, in front of a crowd of 1,500, the fighters traded a flurry of wild punches. Unfortunately, neither boxer managed to land any good ones.

In the third round, Wallitsch flailed away, yet he still failed to connect. He moved in closer for some short, quick jabs and ended up in a clinch. As he broke free, Wallitsch wound up for a haymaker that hit nothing but air.

The force of his missed punch made him lose his balance and he pitched through the ropes head first. His chin slammed on the apron of the ring so hard that Wallitsch was knocked unconscious. The referee counted him out at 2:58 of the third round.

Even though Soni never landed a punch in the round, the record books show that Soni kayoed Wallitsch. But in truth it was Wallitsch who knocked out Wallitsch.

THE TRACK AND FIELD
HALL OF SHAME

Lane Lohr

Pole Vaulter ■ University of Illinois ■ June 5, 1985

A funny thing happened to pole vaulter Lane Lohr on his way over the crossbar—he lost his track shorts.

In the preliminaries of the 1985 NCAA meet in Austin, Texas, Lohr, a junior at the University of Illinois, stole a scene out of a Buster Keaton flick. He had just cleared the bar at seventeen feet, two inches when a gust of wind blew his pole underneath him. As he began to fall, the pole rode up his thigh, slid inside his track shorts, and ripped them right off! Lohr landed in the pit wearing only his jockstrap.

"I was laying there in the pit and the first thing I did was look up and see that the bar was still there," Lohr recalled. "The second thing I did was look down and see that all I had on was my jockstrap. My track shorts were lying beside me, ripped in half."

The crowd was hushed at first, as if no one could believe they were looking at an em-bare-assed pole vaulter. After the reality sank in a few seconds later, the stadium exploded in laughter.

"I didn't know what to do," Lohr said. "Just then an official came running over and brought me a towel. I wrapped it around myself and jumped up and waved to the crowd. Then I went back down the runway because I had to make another jump. I was so into the competition that I would have jumped in my jockstrap if they had let me.

"But a friend of mine who pole-vaulted for Baylor came out of the crowd and offered me his shorts. There's an NCAA rule that you must wear your team uniform. However, a track official told me that I had been granted a special exemption. So right out there in the middle of the field, my friend took off his shorts and gave them to me in exchange for my sweat pants."

Although Lohr placed sixth in the finals with a vault of eighteen feet—good enough for All-America status—he was the butt of jokes for weeks afterward.

How did University of Alabama anchorman Lamar Smith lose a 1,600-meter relay race even though he crossed the finish line first?

The sprinter was disqualified for unsportsmanlike conduct after he taunted his opponents during the race and then mooned the crowd at the Dogwood Relays in Knoxville in 1983.

International Track Association Officials

Los Angeles ■ March 24, 1973

In the inauspicious 1973 debut of indoor professional track, runners nearly came up short in their races because officials ran short of brains.

Thanks to meet workers' bungling, one competitor missed out on a world record.

More than 12,000 fans showed up at the Los Angeles Sports Arena to watch the opening meet of the International Track Association's pro tour. Although the athletes performed professionally, the officials acted amateurishly.

The officials tripped up a run for the record in the 500-meter race. There had been excitement in the air when runners Lee Evans, Larry James, and Vince Matthews announced they were going to attempt to break the old indoor mark of 1:02.9 set by Mal Whitfield in 1953.

After the crack of the starter's gun, Evans burst into the lead and held it with James and Matthews at his heels. As he made the turn to start the final lap, Evans was startled to see that the officials had mistakenly stretched the tape over the finish line one lap too early.

Quickly realizing that they had screwed up, Evans slowed down, hoisted the tape over his head, and kept on running. But James and Matthews thought the race was over and stopped, allowing Evans to breeze to an easy victory. However, because he was hampered by the early tape, Evans missed the record by one second.

When the fans finally figured out what had happened, they let loose with a thunderous chorus of boos while Evans just shook his head in frustration. Disappointed that he didn't break the world record through no fault of his own, Evans said, "When I saw what happened, the first thing I thought of was, 'How am I going to get around that tape?' So I went under it."

As if that wasn't bad enough, a dunderheaded official tried to shortchange the main event—the much-awaited mile run between Jim Ryun and Kip Keino. The two rivals were ready for what promised to be a classic rematch in the 1,760-yard race. What they weren't prepared for was almost running a race of only 1,600 yards. Incredibly, a bumbling official fired his pistol for the gun lap with two laps to go. Keino, in the lead, approached what he thought was the finish line and began to slow down. But then he was waved on for another go-around. Keino hung on to beat Ryun by ten yards in 4:06.

The only real losers in this meet were the officials.

Evans making it under the wire   *Sports Illustrated*/George Long

Amateur Hour

Officials of the 1974 Amateur Athletic Union national indoor championships in New York apparently tried to outdo their pro ITA colleagues in botchery.

For starters, several of the country's longest jumpers complained of gravel in the pit. In fact, defending titlist and Olympic champion Randy Williams stumbled over a rock while warming up and sprained his ankle.

During the women's sprint medley, a vaulter knocked a crossbar onto the track just in time to trip Carmen Brown, who was leading the race.

To cap off this travesty, as another vaulter attempted seventeen feet, the starter of a men's relay fired his pistol a few feet away, sending the startled athlete slithering down his pole.

Jeff Woodard

High Jumper ■ University of Alabama ■ April 24, 1981

Jeff Woodard confused the high jump in a track meet with the high dive in a swim meet.

Woodard, then the NCAA indoor American record holder in the high jump, was competing for the University of Alabama at the Invitational Relays in Walnut, California, when he made his biggest—and most embarrassing—splash ever.

"When I arrived for the meet, I felt fantastic," recalled Woodard. "It was one of those days when just everything was clicking. I felt fast and strong." His mind was so focused on jumping that when he briefly checked out the high jump pit area, he hardly noticed that the pit butted up against the water jump for the steeple race.

"At the time I was at the top of my game and I felt that I could break a record at the meet," he said. Woodard had a feeling it would be an unforgettable day. It was—but not in any way he could have imagined.

"The bar was at seven feet, one and three-fourths inches and I was psyched. On the approach, I went flying. I got one of those once-in-a-lifetime plants and cleared the bar with plenty to spare."

Woodard launched himself with such force that when he landed, he hit the back edge of the pit, rolled over—and went kersplash right into three feet of water in the steeple jump.

"I couldn't believe it," he recalled. "All of a sudden, I was looking up from the bottom of the pit and seeing those ripples on the surface. I told myself, 'Dang, I'm under water!' I came out of the pit and shook off the water. That's when I realized that everyone in the stands and on the field was laughing at me."

Because of this ignominious incident, Woodard became the only high jumper ever to need a snorkle, fins, and mask to clear the bar.

Run for the Rosie's

Running in the footsteps of the infamous Rosie Ruiz, who was caught cheating in both the Boston Marathon and the New York Marathon, dozens of runners at the 1977 Maryland Marathon tried to get away with mass chicanery.

They didn't care about finishing the race. They were only out to get the free souvenir jackets that the sponsors offered to all the starters who finished. Of the 1,707 starters, 1,546 finished—a surprisingly high number that aroused the suspicion of race officials.

An investigation revealed that many runners took advantage of the Maryland course, which was run out and back, unlike the point-to-point Boston Marathon. About nine miles from the starting line, an estimated forty cheaters ducked into a public rest room at various times, stayed a while, and then headed back to the finish line, cutting seven miles off the race. Then they claimed their free jackets.

Joe Holland, cochairman of the event, said after the probe, "We had three people with guilty consciences return the jackets." Apparently, guilt had been outdistanced by the rest of the cheaters.

Oklahoma Christian College's Outdoor Track

1960s–present

The fortunes of athletes competing on Oklahoma Christian College's outdoor track have literally gone with the wind.

It's considered the country's windiest and most treacherous collegiate track because athletes actually get blown away. Gusts have shoved runners out of their lanes, slowed sprinters to a crawl, and stalled pole vaulters in midflight.

OCC happens to sit on a hill overlooking Oklahoma City, the windiest metropolis in America during spring—the height of the outdoor track season. "The wind is so strong around here at that time of year that it can blow you right down and cause you fits," said track coach Randy Heath.

Pole vaulter Jeff Bennett, a five-time All-America and fourth-place finisher in the 1972 Olympic decathlon, learned all about ill winds during his track days at OCC from 1966–70. "The runway only went one way—into the wind," recalled Bennett. "I'd run down the runway, go up, and at about fifteen feet, a twenty-mile-per-hour wind would catch me. I'd start to teeter-totter and then go backwards. I'd fall back on the runway, land on my feet, and roll into a back somersault to soften the impact."

Pole vaulters haven't been the only ones stopped in midair by big blows. The wind plays havoc with the long jumpers, too. Strong gusts sweeping down the plain have pushed slightly built milers and small sprinters right out of their lanes. The quarter-milers also have cast their fate to the wind—and lost. The traditional gut-it-out area for 440 men is the last one hundred yards. At OCC, that area starts at the second curve—the windiest spot on the windiest track. For the athletes, sprinting full tilt into a swirling gust at the second curve is like running into an invisible wall.

"The wind has also scraped most of the cinder right off our track," said Coach Heath. "We're almost down to the bedrock now."

There hasn't been a varsity meet held at OCC since March 9, 1985. Why? The answer, my friend, is blowin' in the wind.

THE HIGH SCHOOL
SPORTS HALL OF SHAME

Homer (Illinois) High vs. Georgetown (Illinois) High

Basketball ■ March 6, 1930

In the most shameful high school basketball game ever played, Georgetown defeated Homer, 1–0.

Most of the four hundred fans would have relished a game decided by a single point, not one that *tallied* a single point. Maybe if the spectators had been Eskimos, they could have appreciated the deep-freeze tactics. The way Georgetown froze the ball, the game might as well have been played at the North Pole rather than in the central Illinois town of Westville, where this contest set a record low in scoring.

Georgetown guard Mike Spasavich became the game's high —and only—scorer when he sank a free throw early in the first period. After Homer missed a shot, Georgetown grabbed the rebound and then sat—literally—on the lead. The team made no further effort to score. Homer didn't help matters any when it played along with the stall.

From the first quarter through the second, third and most of the fourth periods, Georgetown held the ball. The two guards sat on the floor and rolled the ball back and forth to each other. Their teammates talked among themselves, chatted with the spectators, made dates, and did everything but play basketball.

Meanwhile, the Homer players, under orders by their coach, Merle Ririe, retired to their end of the court and sat on the floor. The officials were so bored they went into the bleachers and read the newspaper.

It wasn't until there were only three minutes left in the game that Coach Ririe roused his players out of their slumber and ordered them to break up the stall. But by then it was too late. Even if Homer had scored, most of the fans would have missed it—they had dozed off.

Earnie Seiler

Football Coach ■ Miami (Florida) High ■ November 22, 1924

Football coach Earnie Seiler never tried to break the rules. He merely tried to test their elasticity.

The sneakiest play he ever devised came during the 1924 season when he was coaching at Miami High. He took advantage of the team's unique football field—it had a palm tree standing on the twenty-yard line, fifteen yards in from the sideline.

The tree couldn't be cut down because the owner of the land, Florida East Coast Railroad, donated the property to the school under the strict proviso that not a single coconut palm would be removed. Somehow, Seiler managed to lay out a gridiron among the many palms with only that single tree growing in the field of play.

He waited for the season's biggest game—a contest against Palm Beach High—to spring his trick play. On the kickoff, Miami appeared to have only ten men on the field. Actually, the eleventh player, speedy halfback Ray Carter, was hiding from the Palm Beachers behind the palm tree. The kickoff went to star runner Warner Mizell on the ten-yard line and he headed upfield to the palm tree. As he ran by, he handed the ball off to Carter and, in the same motion, whipped off his leather helmet and threw it to the ground several yards away from the tree. His teammates yelled, "Fumble!" and dove on the helmet, suckering the Palm Beach players to leap into the pile-up.

Meanwhile, Carter stayed hidden from view as the opposing team ran by. He was supposed to count to five, then come out from behind the tree and run like hell. On the sideline, Seiler was counting to himself, and when he reached five, Carter still had not emerged. "Gawdamighty, he can't count!" the coach shouted. But just then, Carter peeked out from behind the palm tree, saw that nobody noticed him, and scampered downfield the entire eighty yards for a touchdown.

The Palm Beach coach charged across the field, followed closely by dozens of Palm Beach fans. "I protest! I protest!" he screamed in rage. "It's against the rules."

Seiler smiled and in a polite, calm voice said, "Show me in the rule book where it says you can't have a palm tree on the football field." The touchdown stood.

Seiler's imaginative coaching sometimes backfired. To help his quarterback Cedric "Froggy" Buchanan select the proper plays, the coach used visual aids. He lined up three buckets on the sideline at midfield. If Seiler tipped pail No. 1, it was the signal to run. Pail No. 2 meant pass, and pail No. 3 signified punt. Once, when his team had driven to the opponent's eighteen-yard line, Seiler wanted Froggy to pass, but the coach mistakenly knocked over the third pail. Froggy stared quizzically at the coach and then dutifully punted the ball out of the end zone and into the second-floor window of the building across the street.

Why did the referee and opposing players shake Dee Dee Neill's hand when she made a free throw?

She scored her team's only point of the game. With less than a minute left in a 1977 girls' basketball game against LeRoy (Kansas) High, Dee Dee, of Quenemo (Kansas) High, sank a foul shot to cut LeRoy's final margin of victory to 83–1.

Ed Myers

Catcher ■ Fredonia (Arizona) High ■ April 25, 1981

Of all the chicanery attempted in high school baseball games, none was more hilariously devious than the potato trick.

It was pulled off by Ed Myers, catcher for Fredonia (Arizona) High. He was taught the scam by his coach, Clint Long, who swore that it once happened in the minors.

Before his team's game against Ash Fork (Arizona) High, Myers bought a potato the size of a baseball for twenty-two cents. Then he stuffed it in his pocket as he took the field in the bottom of the first inning.

"We were already ahead 7–0 and I thought that now was as good a time as any to try the trick," recalled Myers. "So we walked their star hitter, Bill Robertson, and let him steal second and third. We got him cocky and he took a big lead off third. As soon as I caught the next pitch, I whipped out the potato and deliberately fired it over the third baseman's head." When Robertson saw what he thought was the ball sailing down the left-field line, he trotted toward home for what looked like a certain run. But then Myers met him about a third of the way up the line and tagged him out with the ball. "Boy, was he surprised!" said Myers.

"The potato shattered on impact and our leftfielder picked up the pieces and tried to eat all the evidence. I never thought the play could work so well. Our whole team just cracked up."

Not everyone was laughing. A stunned Robertson demanded "Where'd you get that ball?" The home plate umpire scratched his head and said, "Something's wrong here." And Ash Fork coach Lynn Painter, who finally figured out that his team had been duped by the "this-spud's-for-you" trick, protested the play. But Coach Clint Long stumped the huddled umpires by asking, gloatingly, "Is there anything in the rule book that says you can't throw a potato into left field?" To keep the peace, Long eventually relented and allowed the home plate umpire to reverse the call and let Robertson score.

After the game, which Fredonia won 18–7, Ash Fork fans had a little surprise of their own for the winning team—they splattered the Fredonia bus with bananas.

The great potato scam left others fried as well. The Arizona Interscholastic Association put the whole team on probation. "The officials wanted to put a stop to this sort of trickery right away," said Myers. "They had visions of catchers lugging gunny sacks full of potatoes and of mashed potatoes covering the field."

Larry Canaday

Football Coach ■ Eau Gallie (Florida) High ■ 1976–80

It was enough to make you croak. To stir his high school football team into a frenzy, coach Larry Canaday took the disgusting approach —he bit the heads off live frogs.

"The kids loved it," said the coach of the Eau Gallie High School Commodores of central Florida. "They would say, 'Look how wild the coach is. Let's get wild, too.' I did it so our kids would get up for games."

Canaday said he started his pep talk à la toad during practice one day when he tried to fire up one of his linebackers. "I told him, 'Son, you've got to get mad and mean when you're in a game so they won't mess around with you,' " Canaday recalled. "I happened to look down and see this frog. So I grabbed it and told my player, 'You gotta get mean like this.' Then I just bit its head off and spit it out. That kid's eyes got big as saucers.

"After that, the players started bringing me frogs. Why, even parents were sending me frogs. Sometimes, the kids tried to get me to bite the head off a snake. I wouldn't do it because I was afraid they'd bring me a rattler. Frogs don't taste good at all. But they're better than toads, which I don't like at all because they make your lips numb."

Although Canady refused to say how many frogs' heads he had bitten off, he admitted, "You can say that I did my part to hold down the frog population of central Florida—significantly."

When word of his motivational decapitations hit the news wires, many people were hopping mad, and school authorities ordered the coach to stop. "Animal lovers were writing me nasty letters saying how bad I was," said Canaday. "Then some kindergarten teacher who didn't know a damn thing about football called me. She got on me because she had been teaching her kids how to be kind to animals. But you know who were the worst complainers of all? Those damn vegetarians!"

Waverly (Ohio) High Basketball Team

February 19, 1982

In the worst start ever in high school basketball, the Waverly (Ohio) Tigers trailed 7–0 before they even got the chance to touch the ball!

"I suppose I have to take the blame for this," recalled Tom Monroe, a Waverly teacher who acted as the official scorekeeper for the game with the visiting Athens (Ohio) High Bulldogs. "Gabby Smith, our coach at Waverly, had a superstition that only he could put the names and numbers in the official scorebook. Somehow, when he entered the names of his players, he put in the numbers of their away uniforms, which are odd numbers, rather than the even numbers of their home uniforms. I didn't bother to check before the game because our players were still wearing their warmups.

"When the game was about to begin, the scorer for Athens noticed that the uniform numbers were wrong and informed the referee. By then, it was too late for us to do anything about it."

Following the rules, the ref assessed one technical foul before play began against each of the Waverly starters for wearing the wrong numbers. Athens' star shooter, Steve Bruning, made all five of the resulting free throws. Because of the technicals, there was no game-opening jump ball. Instead, the Bulldogs were given the ball out of bounds. Three seconds later, Athens' Mike Croci made a basket on the inbounds play. That made the score 7–0 before the Tigers could even touch the ball.

"The whole game went downhill after that," said Monroe. "I felt bad for the team. As for me, I was rooting for Athens to win by more than seven points." Monroe got his wish. The Bulldogs ripped the Tigers 72–49.

Why did the fans of Big Bay De Noc (Michigan) High celebrate when their team scored a touchdown in the final minute of the final game of the 1979 season in a 34–8 loss?

It was the first time the team had scored in sixteen games. Although they lost their twenty-fifth straight game, the Black Bears of Big Bay De Noc finally broke their streak of having been shut out in fifteen consecutive games, during which they were outscored 830–0.

Butch Ross

Quarterback ■ Shawnee Mission (Kansas) South High
November 13, 1981

With five seconds to play and his Shawnee Mission (Kansas) South High Raiders leading 24–21, quarterback Butch Ross merely had to take the snap and fall on the ball to wrap up the win in a big state regional play-off game.

Yet, in his joy over the team's apparent victory, Ross simply forgot how to execute football's simplest play.

Taking the snap at the forty-yard line of the archrival Shawnee Mission West Vikings, Ross turned and retreated toward his own goal and happily watched the final seconds tick off. Then, in celebration,

Ross started shaking the hands of his teammates while cheering South High fans charged out onto the field.

But although there was no time left on the clock, there was still enough time for Ross to goof up. He never bothered to down the ball!

West High safety John Reichart was smart enough to realize that the ball was still in play because Ross's knee had yet to touch the ground. So Reichart alertly raced up to the unsuspecting Ross, snatched the ball from him at the twenty-five-yard line, and ran into the end zone. The officials immediately signaled a touchdown for West. Ross's blunder had turned a sure 24–21 South victory into a stunning 27–24 season-ending defeat. The once-ecstatic South crowd turned mum from shock while the losing players hurled their helmets down in disgust.

"I told him [Ross] to down the ball," South High coach John Davis ruefully told the press after the game. "I told him to down it, and he didn't do it." What Ross did do was prove that the game is never over until it's over.

White Swan (Washington) High vs. Highland (Washington) High

Wrestling Match ■ January 28, 1982

It was the most bizarre wrestling match in high school history. Not a single take-down or pin. Not a single grunt or groan. That's because the entire wrestling competition between the Washington state schools of White Swan and Highland turned into a surfeit of forfeits.

Both teams had trouble fielding entrants in all thirteen weight classes. So no one seemed surprised when White Swan showed up with only six wrestlers while Highland had just five on hand. But what surprised everyone was that none of the White Swan boys was in the same weight class as any of the Highland boys. That meant no matches could take place.

Because of the odds-defying circumstance, the meet was short, sweet—and shameful. White Swan's Donald Weeks stepped forward and had his hand held up by the referee, who declared him the winner by forfeit in the 101-pound class. Next, Highland's Todd Krienke came out and was announced the winner by forfeit in the 108-pound division. And so it went, right up to Highland's Kent

Wilkinson, who was pronounced victorious—by forfeit, of course—in the unlimited-weight class.

With six points awarded for victory in each match, White Swan won the meet 36–30 by virtue of its one extra man.

"We first realized what was happening at the weigh-in," said White Swan coach Lon Henry. "We couldn't do anything but laugh. I only wished we had known ahead of time because the roads were bad [from a winter storm] and we could have called off the match."

That would have saved the fifty or so spectators from spending their time and money on watching thirteen matchless matches. Several fans demanded a refund, but Highland High officials declined, claiming they still needed the gate receipts to pay the referee. Not that he did very much.

"As we were about to leave," said Coach Henry, "the ref came over to me and said, 'This has been the easiest match I've ever had.' You sure couldn't dispute that."

THE HALL OF SHAME OF SPORTS THAT DON'T HAVE ENOUGH SHAME TO HAVE THEIR OWN HALL OF SHAME

The Wall Game

Eton College ▪ England ▪ 1841–present

If a plaque were given for the worst spectator sport in the world, it could be hung on The Wall Game. Goals are so rare in this bizarre sporting event that only three have been scored in the last 146 years!

The game is a cross between mud wrestling and soccer. What makes the contest so difficult for fans to watch is that they rarely know where the ball is, nor can they determine the identities of the players once the action begins.

The Wall Game is an annual event played at Eton, the famed English public school. The contest begins at noontime on St. Andrew's Day in late fall. The two teams of ten Eton lads each are made up of the Collegers (the students who live in dormitories) and the Oppidans (students who live in town and not on campus). Their uniforms include jerseys, shorts, and tacky striped long socks that quickly become caked with mud.

The playing field, which usually looks like a boggy moor, measures one hundred meters long and seven meters wide and is bounded on one side by a four-meter-high brick wall. The object of the game is to drive a leather ball, which is about half the size of a soccer ball, along the length of the wall and through a goal that is no larger than an ordinary door. If any defender so much as touches the ball in flight, no goal can be scored.

The rules of the game are rather simple and haven't changed much since records were first kept back in 1841. No hands are permitted to advance the ball, which can only be nudged by feet or knees and cannot be passed from one teammate to another. Most of the game is spent with the players bound tightly in a rugbylike scrum called a "bully." Those players not in contact with the ball try to push the bully forward. And that's about all the spectators ever see—a grunting, muddy mass of humanity moving back and forth only a few feet at a time along a wall. Not exactly spine-tingling, catch-your-breath sports action.

Unseen by the fans is the brutality unleashed by the players within the bully. Although hands cannot touch the ball, they can be used to fend off a competitor. Rules forbid kicking, tripping, or punching, and "any method of play whose sole purpose is to cause pain," but almost anything else goes as long as it is not "violent or dangerous." There is a referee on hand, but he doesn't do much other than make sure no one gets smothered to death. If a player on the bottom of the heap manages to yell "Air!", the game immediately stops so he can be rescued.

The contest used to be much fiercer, according to Wall Game expert F.P.E. Gardner, an Eton professor. "Until relatively recently, it was permissible for the players to clench one fist and use their knuckles to gouge the face and eyes of the opponents," he said. "After a particularly rough game, this sadistic pleasure was outlawed because the Collegers were so disfigured that they could scarcely see out of their bruised eyes to do their university scholarship exams the following day."

Noses still get broken and bodies still get bruised, often by the unlikeliest player. For example, "the Fly," who is usually the smallest player on each team, takes on the role of giving a running commentary on the whereabouts of the ball, which has a way of getting lost even to the players. Making up in viciousness what he lacks in size, the Fly often steps on the opponents' hands and employs other forms of questionable sportsmanship. The Fly, say the rules, may not be swatted.

"No account of the Wall Game would be complete without reference to some of its heroes," said Gardner. "The memory of J.K. Stephen, who played in 1874–76, is toasted every year. He is said to have carried the complete Oppidan bully on his back. Then there was O.W.H. Leese, who sat on the ball, unmoved in the center of the bully, for over twenty-two minutes to prevent a Colleger attack."

Maybe players appreciate such a feat, but it doesn't do much for the spectators—or for the scoring. There hasn't been a goal in more than fifty years. The first one was scored in 1842, the next in 1885, and the last fifty-nine years ago in 1928—an average of one goal about every half century. Is there any doubt that this sporting event is just about pointless?

Czechoslovakian Tandem Cyclists

World Cycling Championships ■ Munich ■ August 22, 1978

Competing as though they used a Hell's Angels' handbook as a training manual, the Czechoslovakian tandem cycling team won the gold medal at the 1978 World Cycling Championships. The win-at-any-cost Czechs copped the coveted prize only by deliberately forcing their American opponents off the steeply banked oval track and into a high-speed crash that destroyed the Yanks' bike.

Incredibly, the Czechs were even further honored for the way they rode their vicious cycle.

The defending world champion Czechs were determined not to lose the best two-out-of-three, 2,000-meter-race final. In the first round, American driver Jerry Ash and stoker Leigh Barczewski had pulled even on the inside with Czech driver Vymazal and stoker Vackar. With no concern for their opponents' safety, the Czechs shoved the Americans right off the banked track at the bottom of the back straight. The U.S. tandem pair careened onto the infield grass at 30 m.p.h. but managed to remain parallel to the track. However, the cold-blooded Czechs stayed even with the Yanks, preventing them from returning to the track—until the right moment.

"They didn't give us the chance to get back onto the track until the next turn, where the track is banked forty-eight degrees," recalled Barczewski. "From the infield, that's like heading straight for a wall. We ran into it head-on."

The front tire blew out, causing the wheel to pretzel. Both cyclists were hurtled onto the wooden track, where they skidded and rolled for about ten yards. Ash suffered a broken shoulder while Barczewski sustained cuts and abrasions.

Officials immediately disqualified the Czechs from the first race only. When the call went out for both teams to line up for the second round, the Americans were too injured and their bike was too damaged to compete. So Barczewski and Ash, through no fault of their own, forfeited the next two races. The unopposed Czechs then leisurely pedaled around the track to claim the gold medal as the outraged crowd barraged them with whistles, jeers, and bottles.

"The entire West German team came over to us and congratulated us," said Barczewski. "They said that as far as they were concerned, we were the world champions."

Because of the fans' mounting anger over the Czechs' tactics, officials postponed the awards ceremony until midnight of the following evening, hoping that things would calm down. Even so, nearly 2,000 people showed up to boo the Czechs.

As if there hadn't been enough injustice, the Czechs not only won the gold medal, they also received another award—for, of all things, good sportsmanship!

Kevin Slaten

Announcer ■ St. Louis Steamers Soccer Team ■ March 13, 1981

As the public address announcer for the St. Louis Steamers of the Major Indoor Soccer League, Kevin Slaten was known as a "homer" who blatantly cheered on the team.

But during a play-off game in 1981, he outdid himself. Slaten got so carried away that he slugged a player from the opposing team! For this transgression, Slaten drew a red card, thus becoming the first announcer in professional sports to get thrown out of a game.

For two years, Slaten's emotional pro-Steamer delivery had been a vocal sideshow at home games in the Checkerdome. Whenever a Steamer scored, Slaten got so excited—firing up the partisan crowd—that referees often had to wait for the fans to quiet down before allowing play to resume.

Referee Heinz Wohlmerath was well aware of Slaten's flamboyant delivery. So minutes before the Steamers' play-off game against the visiting Buffalo Stallions, Wohlmerath told Slaten, "I hear you're a good announcer, but you've got to be impartial. The guests have a right to be treated honestly."

Slaten ignored the ref's caution and soon got caught up in the home-team hysteria that he himself had whipped up over the P.A. system.

With 2:53 left in the first half, Buffalo forward John Dolinsky was called for holding and went to the penalty box, which was located next to the announcer's area. Dolinsky, teed off at Slaten's "homerism," turned to him and shouted, "You're the worst announcer in the league!"

Slaten retorted, "Sit down. You're the guys who gave [Steamers defender Greg] Makowski the cheap shot that knocked him out for the season."

Slaten drawing the wrong card   St. Louis Post-Dispatch/Sam Leone

Dolinsky uttered some more uncomplimentary things about Slaten. So the steamed announcer reached over the glass separating him from the penalty box and punched Dolinsky in the face. Wohlmerath then ran over, held up a red card signifying that Slaten had committed a major infraction, and ejected him from the game.

Wohlmerath said Slaten was thrown out for "vicious contact with a player and for using foul and abusive language." The ref said Slaten "deliberately punched" Dolinsky, adding that such behavior was "bad manners."

Wohlmerath took no action against Dolinsky, who told the press, "Slaten kept taunting me, wanting me to lose my cool. He wanted me to fight, but I just laughed at him and he couldn't handle that."

Slaten never returned to the mike. On orders from steamed-up league commissioner Earl Foreman, the Steamers fired him. Although he lost his job, Slaten gained something more meaningful—entry into The Sports Hall of SHAME.

Wilhelm Steinitz

World Champion Chess Player ■ 1872–94

Alexander Alekhine

World Champion Chess Player ■ 1927–46

Chess champions Wilhelm Steinitz and Alexander Alekhine were not only the world's worst losers but also the world's worst winners. They played chess as if the board were really a battlefield and they were really kings.

The Czechoslovakian-born Steinitz, who played professional chess throughout Europe in the last half of the nineteenth century, was the most despised player who ever lived. He treated opponents as if they were nothing more than pawns who deserved to be captured. He destroyed them not only with his skill but also with his tongue. Once, when a colleague questioned his strategy, Steinitz snapped, "You're like a monkey examining a watch."

Opponents needed more than chess smarts to play Steinitz—they needed boxing gloves. Because he interpreted the most innocent remarks as personal insults, he constantly triggered fights with his colleagues. Known as much for the Steinitz temper as he was for the Steinitz Gambit, the explosive grandmaster turned chess halls into mine fields. None of his opponents ever knew when they would accidentally set him off. During the Paris Tournament in 1867, he blew up over a trivial remark made by his British opponent Joseph Blackburne. In a rage, Steinitz spat in his face. Blackburne, who was no white knight himself, promptly picked up the short, squat megalomaniac and threw him right out the window!

Steinitz was a great substandard bearer for Alexander Alekhine, a Russian-born grandmaster who settled in Paris and terrorized international chess competition during the first half of this century. His opponents faced the fury of hell after those rare moments when they uttered "checkmate." That little word unleashed a volcano. Once, after he was forced to surrender in a major tournament, a raging Alekhine grabbed his lead-weighted king and hurled it like a beanball across the room, nearly braining a referee who ducked just in time.

Alekhine didn't only throw chess pieces. He also was known to fling furniture in his hotel room after a loss. Chess patrons learned never to invite Alekhine to their homes because they valued their furniture. They also valued their money and wives, both of which he often attempted to steal.

In his last major public appearance, Alekhine got rip-roaring drunk during a simultaneous exhibition in Spain where he was playing several games at once. In one game that he seemed sure to lose, he whipped out a new strategy for his famed Alekhine Defense. He stood up and peed on the board.

Chuck Ryan

Ski Jumper ■ Duluth Invitational ■ January 25, 1959

For ski jumpers, it's always "Look, Ma, no hands!" For jumper Chuck Ryan, it was "Look, Ma, no skis!"

Ryan hadn't planned on it, but he set the unofficial record for the longest ski jump without skis.

More than 2,500 fans were on hand during the 54th annual Duluth Invitational ski jumping championships in Fond du Lac, Minnesota, hoping to witness at least one jump for the record book. What they saw was one for The Sports Hall of SHAME.

Ryan, a nine-year veteran with the St. Paul Ski Club, should have brought a parachute before starting down the sixty-meter slide, because when he hit the takeoff, both his skis flew off his feet. Soaring through the air for 148 feet, Ryan cursed himself for using new skis without testing the bindings. Then he told himself to prepare for a rough landing. He hit the snow at an angle and skidded another one hundred feet before coming to a stop, unhurt.

"I just jumped out of my skis," said the twenty-six-year-old skier. "I wasn't really scared, but I kept thinking that I better not land on my feet and risk breaking my legs. So I went in like a baseball player sliding into second."

The worst shame of all is that no one wrote a song about Ryan's weird jump. The ditty could have been called, "The Flight of the Bumble Skis."

Wrestlezania

It's hard to believe that in any collegiate sport, a team can get a worse score than zero. But Loyola College of Baltimore managed.

In a dual wrestling meet against the University of Maryland at Baltimore County in 1977, Loyola lost 51 to –1.

To come up with that rare score, the defeated grapplers needed the help of their coach, Andy Amasia. While Loyola was losing all ten of its matches, the coach took out his frustrations on the referee by jawing at him. The ref responded by slapping Loyola with a misconduct foul that called for a deduction of one point. Since Loyola was shut out, its final tally was –1!

University of Miami Swim Team

February 3, 1978

If only members of the University of Miami swim team had looked before they leaped, the Hurricanes would have swum clear of their most deplorable pool performance ever.

The largest crowd of the year packed the bleachers to cheer Miami in its dual meet against the favored arch rival University of Florida Gators. Going into the final event, the 400-yard freestyle relay, Miami trailed 54–52 and needed to win the relay in order to win the meet.

With fans shouting themselves hoarse, the Miami anchor hit the finish wall in 3:06.05, narrowly touching out his Gator rival by just twelve hundredths of a second. By winning the race, the Hurricanes had picked up seven points to beat Florida, 59–54. At least that's what most everyone thought, especially several deliriously happy Miami swimmers who celebrated by plunging into the pool—some while still wearing their sweats and sneakers.

Unfortunately, the splash party was a bit premature—and definitely costly. Only after the Hurricanes were whooping it up in the pool did the officials notice that the anchor on Florida's hopelessly outmanned B relay team was still poking along in the water. When the laggard finally finished, in 3:31.45, the crowd's rejoicing was torpedoed and silenced by an official announcement.

Because its swimmers had gone into the water while the race was technically still in progress, Miami's relay team had broken the rules and was disqualified. The seven points the Hurricanes had earned were taken away and given to Florida. Miami lost the meet, 61–52.

Similar fates have sunk the fortunes of swim teams, but none so drastic as the disaster that befell the Hurricanes. At the 1971 NCAA championships, for example, Indiana's 800-yard freestyle relay team was disqualified when swimmers (and future Olympic gold medalists) Mark Spitz and John Kinsella reentered the pool too soon. But Indiana already had piled up enough points to win the championship anyway.

Miami had no extra lifesaving points to save its victory from slipping away. "It was quite a shock," recalled Bill Diaz, the Miami swim coach at the time. After the debacle, he made sure it would never happen again. "Before the end of any big race," said Diaz, "I always sent one of my assistant coaches up to the edge of the pool deck with orders to grab any overly enthusiastic swimmer who looked like he was ready to jump into the pool too early."

Kia (aka Paul) Sladeski

Rodeo Barrel Racer ■ 1984

Rodeo cowgirl Kia Sladeski was most definitely a breed apart from her competitors.

By winning the most points and money in barrel racing—the only rodeo event expressly for women—Kia was named the American Rodeo Association's 1984 Rookie Cowgirl of the Year. Yep, the rodeo folks were mighty proud of how the tenderfoot filly managed to lasso that honor. Of course, that's before they discovered they had been hornswoggled.

You see, Kia was no cowgirl. Kia, it turned out, was a cow*boy*.

Word came from her/his hometown of Pine Bush, New York. "I was originally sent out with a photographer to do this local-girl-makes-good story," recalled Billy House, reporter for the Middletown *Times Herald-Record*. "We thought she was awfully homely, but who are we

Sladeski, a breed apart from the rest   *Middletown Times Herald-Record*

to say? We ran the photo and story, and the next day we were flooded with calls telling us she was really a he."

Kia Sladeski was actually Paul W. Sladeski, female impersonator, exotic dancer, and male prostitute. "We had been wondering what happened to him," Newburgh, New York, police detective Frank DeLuca told the press. "Nobody had seen him around for some time. Paul Sladeski and Kia Sladeski are one and the same." DeLuca arrested Sladeski in 1977 for male prostitution. Sladeski, known on the street as Kia, pleaded guilty to the charge and was sentenced to sixty days in jail.

When Kia was asked by the *Times Herald-Record* if she/he knew Paul Sladeski, Kia at first answered "No," then said, "Yes, he's my brother . . . No, he's my father."

Rodeo association president Al Samuels called a board meeting to discuss whether Sladeski should receive the silver belt buckle emblematic of the rookie cowgirl honor. "I certainly can't go ahead and award a Rookie Cowgirl of the Year buckle to someone who may be a cowboy," Samuels told the press. Sladeski solved the dilemma by relinquishing the title and resigning from the association.

But for a year, Kia Sladeski had the rodeo folks over a barrel.

El Salvador   Honduras

June–July, 1969

To be up in arms over a hostile soccer rivalry is one thing. But to take up arms is quite another. Nationalistic fervor was so intense during the World Cup competition in 1969 that El Salvador and Honduras extended their clashes from the soccer field to the battle field.

A three-game World Cup series between the two feuding Central American neighbors triggered an infamous and short-lived armed conflict known as the "Soccer War."

After Honduras won the first game 1–0 at home, fans from both sides skirmished. The riotous scene was repeated the following week when Honduras was beaten 3–0 in El Salvador. Outraged by the defeat, Hondurans began attacking Salvadoran immigrants who had been living in Honduras. By now, tensions were too high to play the third and deciding game in either nation, so World Cup officials scheduled it in neutral territory—Mexico City.

That did little to temper passions. In fact, the situation grew even worse because the sister republics broke off diplomatic relations over the games. Less than twenty-four hours later, under the watchful eyes of 1,700 Mexican policemen, El Salvador downed Honduras 3–2.

The game may have ended in embraces and handshakes between the two teams, but it also inflamed enough hostility to ignite a war. Fortunately, since the soldiers displayed less combat skill than the players did soccer skill, the Western Hemisphere was spared open warfare.

Entire companies of soldiers deserted at the first whiff of gun powder. The adversaries were armed with hand-me-down U.S. Army rifles and machine guns, a few bazookas, mortars, and howitzers. Salvadoran soldiers managed to advance across the Honduran border with only the help of Texaco road maps. The rickety Salvadoran air force—mostly relics from World War II junk yards—could barely get off the ground. Honduras sent up creaky old C-47 cargo planes that were converted into bombers by having crewmen toss explosive charges from open side doors.

Unlike the World Cup matches, the Soccer War ended in a tie. Both sides lost.

Istvan Gaal

Canadian National Soccer League Player ■ 1971

Istvan Gaal was such a lousy soccer player that he was traded to a rival team for a soccer ball!

"I think it was a very fair trade," said John Fischer, president of the Kitchener Concordia Kickers of the Canadian National Soccer League. "Both teams got what they wanted."

Gaal was a player whose skills apparently couldn't be measured by money. There was no cash involved in the swap with the Toronto Hungarians. It was a straight player–ball deal.

"We didn't give him away for nothing," Fischer insisted. "We got a regulation National Soccer League ball in return. They go for $27.50."

Long before the trade, Gaal, a twenty-one-year-old Hungarian defector who claimed he had scored thirty-one goals in forty-four games back in his native country, had been considered a prize catch. In fact, the Kickers went to extraordinary means to sign him—they kidnapped him. Gaal had agreed to terms with Toronto, but while he was standing on a Toronto street corner with a team representative, a black car screeched to a halt in front of them. Two men hustled Gaal into their car and roared off to Kitchener, where he was persuaded to sign with the Kickers.

Unfortunately, he turned out to be a big disappointment, said Fischer. "He had a few moves, but he looked bad. At first, we thought he was holding back. He had just arrived in a new country and couldn't speak the language. We thought he'd be okay once he adjusted. But he never improved."

Gaal was so bad that he couldn't even make it as a substitute on the Kickers, who were in thirteenth place in the fourteen-team league. So a deal was struck with Toronto.

Recalled Fischer, "The Toronto team said to me, 'Why don't you just release the guy to us?' I said, 'Hell no, I'm not going to give him away for nothing. You send me that soccer ball.' They said they would. And they did.

"The trade wasn't all that unique," added Fischer. "I went checking through the records and found that a hockey player was once traded for a pair of nets."

Pembroke State College Baseball Team

1982–83

Pembroke State College of North Carolina holds the title as the cheapest, most penny-pinching college baseball team in the country.

Pembroke first gained national recognition for parsimony when its players walked off the field of a tie game so they wouldn't miss out on a free meal.

On March 2, 1982, Pembroke State hosted North Carolina at Charlotte in a game that was knotted 8–8 after nine innings. But before the contest headed into the tenth frame, Pembroke coach Harold Ellen pulled his team off the field. Pointing to his watch, which read 6:25 p.m., he explained to his disbelieving opponents that the school cafeteria was about to close. "We don't have the money like the big schools have," Ellen said, "and I can't afford to send them to McDonald's." So he hustled his players off to the cafeteria because if they didn't get there in time, they wouldn't get a free supper.

"Some people around here got a little upset," admitted Gary Spitler, Pembroke's sports information director. "Several alumni sent in a dollar or two to contribute to the food fund. McDonald's sent us a bunch of complimentary coupons and said, 'The next time you get hungry and can't finish a game, come in here and eat.'"

A year later, on March 13, 1983, Pembroke's team behaved as if it were owned by Silas Marner. Playing at home against the Princeton Tigers in a late-afternoon game, Pembroke rallied to tie the score at 4–4 after six innings. But then Pembroke called the game on account of darkness—even though Pembroke's field had lights.

To the stunned amazement of the Princeton players, they were informed that Pembroke turned on the lights only for night games and "important games" such as those with fellow members of the Carolinas Conference.

Said Gary Spitler ruefully, "The minute we called the game, I knew people were going to say, 'There they go again.'"

Lucky Maury

Greyhound ▪ Hollywood Greyhound Track ▪ January 19, 1978

In greyhound racing, dogs are trained to dash around the track and chase a fleeing mechanical rabbit that they can never catch. Greyhound Lucky Maury thought all this running for nothing was a bunch of puppy-cock. So he decided to take a different route. He turned tail and ran the *opposite* way—and ambushed the onrushing bunny!

Lucky Maury was only a ten-to-one shot to win the fifth race at Hollywood Greyhound Track in Florida. But after he broke late from the starting box, he looked like a million-to-one loser. He took two gallops down the track and screeched to a halt as if he wanted nothing more to do with an event that had gone to the dogs.

Rather than just give up and head back to the paddock with his tail between his legs, the two-year-old racer took matters into his own paws.

Lucky Maury made a U-turn on the track, eluded a frantic patrol judge who tried to grab him, and scampered off in the opposite direction. He finally met up with the speeding bunny head-on at the clubhouse turn. Lucky Maury clamped his jaws on the mechanical rabbit, ripped it, and let the fur fly. When the other dogs caught up, it was hare today, gone tomorrow.

Such a scandalous flouting of the rules caused fans to howl with laughter. Management had no choice but to refund all $47,000 that had been wagered on the race.

Lucky Maury ended up in the doghouse. A week after his run to shame, he was put in a non-betting schooling (or practice) race for a refresher course on greyhound-rabbit etiquette.

WHO ELSE BELONGS IN THE SPORTS HALL OF SHAME?

Do you have any nominations for The Sports Hall of SHAME? Give us your picks for the most shameful, embarrassing, deplorable, blundering, and boneheaded moments in sports history. Here's your opportunity to pay a lighthearted tribute to the world of athletics.

Those nominations that are documented with the greatest number of facts—such as firsthand accounts or newspaper or magazine clippings—have the best chance of being inducted into The Sports Hall of SHAME. Feel free to send as many nominations as you wish for any sport. (All submitted material becomes the property of The Sports Hall of SHAME and is nonreturnable.) Mail your nominations to:

> The Sports Hall of SHAME
> P.O. Box 6218
> West Palm Beach, FL 33405

THE WINNING TEAM

BRUCE NASH has suffered his share of ignominy in virtually every sport. In his golfing debut, he didn't even make it to the first green—he ran out of balls after shanking eight of them into the water. At the bowling alley, fellow keglers still talk about the time Bruce threw a wild ball that landed in the gutter—of the next lane. While umpiring a kids' sandlot game in his hometown of West Palm Beach, Florida, Bruce's calls so enraged both teams that the players replaced him with the park's groundskeeper in the third inning.

ALLAN ZULLO has turned his athletic life around. He used to be pathetic and bungling. Now he's bungling and pathetic. As a golfer in Palm Beach Gardens, Florida, he often shoots one under—one under a tree, one under a bush, one under the water. He hits his woods great; the problem is getting out of them. On the tennis court, Allan is a C– player whose serves have the hang time of an NFL punt. In softball, he's one of the unluckiest pitchers in the park league—Allan always pitches when the other team scores lots of runs.

Hall of SHAME curator BERNIE WARD learned all about shame in high school in Norton, Kansas. He managed to pin himself in a wrestling match when he tripped backwards over his own feet. After watching Bernie try out for track, his coach entered him in a new event—javelin-catching.